Singing MATTERS

PATRICK ALLEN

Heinemann

Singing

MATTERS

Heinemann

Heinemann is an imprint of Pearson Education Limited, a company incorporated in England and Wales, having its registered office at Edinburgh Gate, Harlow, Essex CM20 2JE.
Registered company number: 872828

Heinemann is the registered trademark of Pearson Education Ltd.

First published 1997

10 09 10

British Library Cataloguing in Publication Data
A catalogue record for this book is available from the British Library

ISBN: 978 0 435810 15 3

Typeset and designed by Artistix, Thame, Oxon
Music typesetting by Halstan & Co., Amersham, Bucks
Printed in the UK by Ashford Colour Press Ltd.
Cover photos by Chris Honeywell, Zefa and Della Robbia – The Bridgeman Art Library/Museo Dell Opera Del Duomo

Acknowledgements

The author would like to dedicate this pack to the pupils of Ifield Community College, Crawley and would like to thank Angeline Bell and Margaret Vodden of Ifield Community College, Kath Penny of Bewbush Middle School, Anne and Alun Lewis, Gillian and Graham Pearson, Luke and Sarah Trotter, Larry Gordon, Rosie Owen and the members of Village Harmony for their ideas, help and support in the preparation of this pack.

The publishers would like to thank the following for permission to reproduce copyright material:
At the hop words and music by A. Singer, J. Medora and D. White © 1957 (Renewed) Arc Music Corporation. All rights reserved on pp. 47–8; *Three lions* Music by Ian Broudie. Words by David Baddiel & Frank Skinner. Published by Chrysalis Music Ltd. on pp. 71–3; *Flower of Scotland* by The Corries © The Corries (Music) Ltd. on p. 170; *Rock around the clock* by Jimmy de Knight and Max C Freedman © Edward Kassner Music Co. Ltd. on pp. 46–8; *Wimoweh* by Solomon Linda: Paul Campbell © 1951 & 1952 Folkways Music Publishers Inc., New York, USA. Assigned to Cromwell Music Ltd., London SW10 0SZ. International copyright secured. All Rights Reserved. Used by Permission on pp.64–5; *All I have to do is dream* words and music by Boudleaux Bryant © Copyright 1958 House of Bryant Publications, USA. Acuff-Rose Music Limited, London W1. Used by permission of Music Sales Limited. All Rights reserved. International copyright secured on pp. 99–100; *Stand by me* words and music by Ben E. King, Jerry Leiber and Mike Stoller © 1961 (Renewed) Jerry Leiber Music, Mike Stoller Music and Unichappell Music inc. All rights outside of the United States and Canada controlled by Jerry Leiber Music and Mike Stoller Music. All rights reserved. On p. 101; *Barbara Anne* words and music by Fred Fassert © Copyright 1961 Longitude Music Company, USA. Windswept Pacific Music Limited for the UK and Eire. Used by permission of Music Sales Limited. All Rights reserved. International copyright secured on pp. 87–9; *Love is all around* words and music by Reg Presley © Copyright 1967 Dick James Music Limited, 47 British Grove, London W4. Used by permission of Music Sales Limited. All Rights reserved. International copyright secured on pp. 67–9; *Only you* words and music by Vincent Clarke © Copyright 1982 Sony/ATV Music Publishing, 10 Great Marlborough Street, London W1. Used by permission of Music Sales Limited. All Rights reserved. International copyright secured on pp. 38–40; *Rivers of Babylon* words and music by Farian, Reyam, Dowe and McNaughton © Copyright Far Musikverlag and Beverlys Records for the world. © Copyright 1978 Far Musikverlag Gmbh/Hansa Productions Limited. Blue Mountain Music Limited for the UK and Eire. Used by permission of Music Sales Limited. All Rights reserved. International copyright secured on pp. 80–82; *Wonderwall* words and music by Noel Gallagher © Copyright 1995 Oasis Music/Creation Songs Limited/Sony/ATV Music Publishing, 10 Great Marlborough Street, London W1. Used by permission of Music Sales Limited. All Rights reserved. International copyright secured on pp. 31–3; *Canoe Round* by Margaret Embers McGee from *The Great Rounds Songbook* by Esther Nelson published by Sterling Publishing Co., Blandford Press © Esther Nelson on p. 151; *You are not alone* by R. Kelly © Zomba Music on pp. 114-119.

The publishers have made every effort to trace copyright holders. However, if any material has been incorrectly acknowledged, we would be pleased to correct this at the earliest opportunity.

Contents

Part 1: Singing in the classroom

Part 2: Games, warm-ups and backings

Part 3: Singing projects

Part 4: Rounds, chants and social songs

Rounds

Chants

Social songs

Introduction

Singing is one of the most potent communal, convivial and expressive activities known to humankind, and is an important aspect of all societies throughout the world and throughout history. It improves our confidence and our relations with others and binds groups; it is an important expressive outlet and accompanies some of the most significant moments of our lives. To deny young people the opportunity to sing will hinder their human and social development and imprison their feelings.

As a music teacher in a large comprehensive school, I know that developing good singing in class at Key Stage 3 (S1/S2) is not easy. Like many teachers, I have encountered classes so embarrassed they hardly dare make a sound and others so over-excited they sound like a pub at closing time! Often everything seems to be against achieving the happy medium; not only are many of the voices changing but the image and self-consciousness problems of adolescence begin to take a grip. It just seems so much easier to have them play instruments, to write or listen rather than unleash their voices on the world …

To make matters worse, I have attended many courses on singing in schools which seem to bear no relation to the children I teach. I have been shown anatomical diagrams of the larynx, been told to imagine a string pulling my head up, a hot potato in my mouth and then advised that Britten's *Ceremony of Carols* would be a good way to initiate part-singing in the class. Returning to my school, I wondered if I was the only person whose classes couldn't sing a cathedral choir repertoire. I decided to shelve the advice and begin by studying my pupils rather than high-flown ideas intended for a handful of elite singers. The outcome of these informal researches and my experiences with my classes and other groups of young singers have resulted in *Singing Matters*.

About the pack

Singing Matters is a pack of resources designed for singing at Key Stage 3 (S1/S2). It contains songs, ideas, advice, games, rounds, chants, warm-ups and follow-up work. It assumes that teachers will be working in a variety of circumstances with a wide range of pupils of many different abilities and backgrounds. The pack does not, therefore, propose a sequence of activities to be followed slavishly under all circumstances. Rather it expects that teachers will select those activities and parts of projects which will suit them, the pupils they teach and the general scheme of work followed in their school.

Within each project there are opportunities for widely differentiated activities. For example, the project *Babethandaza* (Project 28) begins with a simple chant accessible to all which can be developed into a more complex four-part harmony singing project. It is therefore important to understand that, while progression has influenced the order of the projects, they are not presented in order of difficulty, since each project can be approached on a variety of levels and used for both progression and differentiation within itself. It would be entirely possible to begin a course with material from project 28 or 30 if it matched your pupils' needs and interests.

It is expected that teachers will return to projects, exploiting fresh challenges within them whilst building on an already established basis. Each project, therefore, contains some material all pupils can manage but many also contain real challenges which will stretch the most able. The pack also allows for opportunities to combine vocal and instrumental work and to integrate singing into a broader scheme of work.

The structure of the pack

The pack is presented in the following way:

- **Part 1** gives guidance on how to encourage singing, outlines some principles underlying the material in the pack, suggests uses for IT and computers with singing and gives general advice on how to use the singing projects provided in Part 3.

- **Part 2** presents warm-up activities, games to encourage singing and scores for backing tracks which may be useful in aural training, improvising and composing.

- **Part 3** contains thirty singing projects arranged to provide a varied, active and enjoyable experience of singing. Each project provides background information, suggests a singing style, explains how to teach the material, how to accompany it and how best to perform it. Suggestions are also made for follow-up work.

- **Part 4** provides a collection of rounds and chants as well as 'social' songs which pupils may find useful outside school.

The aims of the pack

The songs, chants, rounds, ideas, games and activities in this pack have been selected to help singing in schools in the following ways:

- **Creating a social environment for singing** The pack provides a range of games and activities to break the ice socially, and includes a number of songs which pupils will find 'cool' to sing.

- **Integrating singing into the music curriculum** The pack aims to integrate singing into the music curriculum as a whole by providing follow-up activities and by encouraging singing as a normal part of classroom life.

- **Vocal range** The songs in *Singing Matters* are pitched in a range that is comfortable for the majority of pupils, with harmony and extension parts for those with higher or lower voices. Most parts can be sung in any octave.

- **Harmony and part-singing** Many opportunities, of varying complexity, are given for harmony and part-singing.

- **Choice of material** Material has been chosen to appeal to the age group, to cover the requirements of the National Curriculum and Expressive Arts 5–14, to be simple to learn yet provide adequate challenges for the most able, and to represent a wide range of cultures and singing styles.

- **Flexibility** The material is presented for use in a variety of ways and with a wide range of pupils.

- **Improving standards of singing** The pack provides advice on how to improve the quality of singing in class and how best to perform and teach the songs.

Creating a social environment for singing

Singing exposes us. We are *ourselves* the medium and the music. For a group of adolescents where peer group opinion can be everything, this can be an alarming prospect. Often, they would rather blend quietly in with the crowd than have their voices stand out. So the first thing to do is to create an environment where pupils feel it is socially acceptable to be heard singing. The games and activities in Part 2 (pages 12–27) are aimed specifically at this.

Creating a singing environment in the classroom

If there is not much singing in your classes at present and you want this to change quickly, then start with Years 7 and 8. Year 9 will be a big challenge if they are not used to singing. Habits established early will, however, stay with pupils. Gradually build up a repertoire of songs and games to which you can return, including a repertoire of 'partner songs' (Projects 1, 3, 6, 8 and 19) which are an easy way into part-singing. It is important that singing is part of *all* the work you do in music and not a 'special' activity or time filler.

For example, when you are demonstrating or teaching a phrase or melody in any music lesson, sing it rather than play it and get the individual or class to sing it back. Involve poetry, verse, rap and choral speaking in pupils' work. If you are exploring sounds for composition or graphic work, demonstrate and experiment with vocal sounds as well as instrumental. In rhythm work get pupils to make rhythmic sounds with their voices, perhaps imitating percussion instruments or inventing their own sounds. Pupils are often much less inhibited about being creative with their voices than adults are.

Most crucially, *the teacher must sing!* This can be embarrassing at first, particularly if your classroom has been a singing-free zone, but the pupils will sing easily if you do. This doesn't mean you need to be a trained singer with special skills (in fact in some ways it's helpful not to be). It just involves you doing what you are expecting your class to do: singing naturally and easily, without artifice or pretence. So there's no need to put on a special voice or be grand and dramatic. If you can speak to your class, singing to them is a logical next step. So take the plunge if you haven't already, and sing!

Creating a singing environment in school

Singing in school will be a low status activity for most pupils if it is the preserve of a small number of clever ones who can read music. It will be a high status activity if it is fun, open to all, caters for all sorts of voices and has the captain of the rugby team as well as the library monitor in it.

Singing should be associated with a range of musical styles, including pop music, and should be available to pupils in more imaginative contexts than just a choir which stands in rows. In fact to some pupils the very words 'choir' and 'singing' can create revulsion, due to associations with formalized and dreary performances of music they could neither feel nor understand. So, why not have a pop concert to celebrate the culture they enjoy, or start a harmony gospel group, or set up workshops with African music? Once you've kindled their enthusiasm for singing they will much more readily join a choir.

Vocal range

Whole class singing at this age is made more difficult by the diverging vocal ranges of the class and the challenge of establishing what is a median vocal range for unison singing. Most song books for the 11–14 range are pitched far too high, usually for soprano. It is astonishing that books are still being published with this false ideal of young people's singing and with no reference to the young people themselves.

As early as 1955, Charles Cleall had noted from surveys in the UK and US that 57 per cent of 12-year-old girls and 60 per cent of boys could sing as low as E below middle C, whereas only 50 per cent of the age group could reach D, an octave above middle C with any confidence. Despite being a church musician himself, he deplored the way so many young people were deemed failures because they did not match the ideal of a child treble or soprano. He says, 'It seems we have paid too little attention to what our young people *can* do and too much to what our cherished tradition says they ought to do … our present pitch plays into the hands of a minority who like to *crow over others* … tone deafness is actually *caused* by musicians, since standard pitch only suits a trained and selected minority.' He also writes of the damaging effects of forcing young voices to sing too high and notes the discomfort his singers created in a hospital with too much high soprano singing.

Cleall's study also noted that nearly 100 per cent of the age group could sing the notes from A below middle C to F above it. With this, and my own experience in mind, the unison singing range of the songs in *Singing Matters* centres on this area. It accommodates changing and changed voices (who will sing an octave lower) and the whole range of girls' voices. It also is a more acceptable sound to this age group, since it corresponds to the range of most pop singers.

It is, however worth noting that:

- the harmony, ostinato and extension parts cater for a wider vocal range
- most parts can be sung or doubled in any octave
- the vocal range which suits this age group may be difficult for some adults to sing
- since most songs can be learned aurally, transposition may simply mean giving a new starting note.

Flexible vocal parts

Melodies, harmonies and bass lines can be sung in any octave, so it's best not to think in terms of SATB, with the tune on top. There may be basses singing the tune and sopranos singing the bass line! In Singing Matters there is much use of parallel harmonies which allow those with higher or lower voices to sing something closely corresponding to the tune in an area of the voice which suits them and which harmonizes with it.

Where should the teacher's voice be pitched?

It is obviously easiest if you pitch your voice in the octave where most pupils will be singing. Some men may find it impossible to sing in this region and will be obliged to sing an octave lower than the majority. This may confuse some pupils who will attempt to sing very low. If this is a problem with the class reinforce your singing with an instrument playing at the correct pitch. I actually sing in a falsetto voice in order to define accurately the range I want. Surprisingly, no one laughs!

'Head' voice versus 'chest' voice

In the arranging of these songs 'head' voice has certainly not been abandoned in favour of 'chest' voice. I have tried to remember that most teachers do not have trainee cathedral choirs in front of them, that there is only an hour per week of music, and that for an increasing number of the class members, as KS3 progresses, there simply is no choice between head and chest voice. Hopefully those pupils whose voices would benefit from stretching upwards will have opportunities beyond the classroom as well as from extension parts in this pack.

Protecting the 'head' voice

Once a class enjoy singing and sing with gusto, there is a danger of 'belt' in the chest register, leaving some voices with a nasty break between head and chest or with pupils straining too high in chest register. It is important to bring the qualities of the head voice into the lower notes and to keep the higher notes strong, for those who have them.

A descending scale starting on B above middle C will encourage appropriate pupils to take the head voice down to the lower areas. See how low they can take their head voice. This scale can then be started on C, C# and D. Such pupils should also be encouraged to move into head when they reach about F or G above middle C.

Organizing singing in the classroom

Pupil conduct

Whilst we want spirited and energetic singing, it also needs to be controlled and disciplined. For this reason there must be a clear code of conduct in the classroom, particularly concerning silence at an agreed cue and respect for others and their work. Singing, like percussion work, is full of pitfalls and problems if these ground rules are not established early on. It is well worth spending the first few lessons of any year establishing very clear parameters for behaviour. Many of the activities at the early stage are based around pupils obeying instructions, often by way of imitation games rather than lengthy rules and instructions. These are a non-verbal way of communicating control and sensitivity as well as instrumental and vocal techniques.

Imitation games

I often start lessons with an activity involving the immediate copying of what I do. This is not quite the same as echo-clapping or singing, where there is a space to respond. There must be complete silence and all eyes must be on the teacher. Clap once: they clap with you; move your hands to any position: they move with you. Next clap at a variety of speeds and volumes with the class imitating exactly what you do *as you do it*.

This is a mirroring activity which puts them entirely in sync with you and makes them very aware. Over time this develops into a situation where they will, on request, immediately imitate absolutely anything you do, including vocal sounds and movement. This may seem a rather Pavlovian technique, but it works well and initiates important habits of observation and listening early on. It also puts the teacher in charge. These activities are more fully developed in the games section (see pages 12–27).

Organizing class singing

The pupils should be prepared for flexible classroom arrangements from early on and should be trained to be adaptable and co-operative, especially when re-arranging the furniture, handing out and collecting sheets of music and moving to different parts of the room for various activities. Always be clear about what you want them to do and where you want them to go, and give them adequate time to achieve it. The human organizational elements of music lessons are crucial and should not be rushed or fudged. My school uses a system of rewards (merit points and stickers) to commend social behaviour, good work and progress. I find them useful.

Where to organize singing

The material in this pack is for use in and beyond the music classroom. Much works well in the classroom but some full arrangements are best done with a junior choir and some of the part-singing will be suitable for large groups, such as combined classes or assemblies.

Always ensure you have adequate space for the activity you are organizing and that the room is well ventilated and not too hot. It is important that pupils often stand to sing, but they must have chairs available since singing can be a tiring activity.

Arranging the pupils

You must be prepared to be flexible with your classroom arrangements for singing: pupils may be in pairs, groups, rows or in a circle. Singing will also take place as a part of composing and instrumental work so it is best not to associate it with one particular room plan.

Games, warm-ups, chanting and call and response are often best done in a circle, either seated or standing with the chairs and tables out of the way. Rhythm games are also best done in a circle and these should be connected with voice work from an early stage. If you are using your computer to provide a backing track (see page 8), have it and the speaker suitably positioned. Be part of the circle yourself and don't hide behind anything. All sorts of things can be sung unaccompanied in a circle: chants, rhythms, rounds, football songs, themes from the classics, nursery rhymes, songs from musicals and chart hits.

For other activities you may want pupils seated neatly around you while you play an instrument to teach or accompany a song. Always decide how you want the furniture arranged before the class do, and always set a deadline to achieve it. You should be able to see the whole class whilst playing and be constantly assessing pupils' progress.

Structuring the lesson

1 **Preparation**
Plan the lesson carefully and have at hand adequate resources including the relevant music sheets, any instruments, the computer, a tape recorder and a tape for the particular class you are teaching. You may have to ask the class to arrange the furniture as they arrive if it has not been done before the lesson.

2 **Warm-up**
It is best to start the lesson with games, chants or warm-ups and some material with which pupils are already familiar. However, don't exhaust them on this. The idea is to warm them up and energize them for the main activity. Try to work ideas and musical phrases from the main activity into the warm-ups. Some games may over-excite pupils, so carefully choose an activity or song which will calm them. *Only you* (Project 4) is an excellent song for calming a group down and creating a softer vocal tone.

3 **Main task**
After 5 minutes or so of warm-ups you will probably want to move on to the main activity. Spend no more than 15 minutes teaching them new material or you will lose the pupils' attention. Use the remaining time to improve their performance of the new piece(s) and to record it.

4 **Recording, evaluating and follow-up work**
Spend time evaluating, discussing and responding to the main activity. This may include moving on to the follow-up work provided.

5 **Re-arranging the room and resources**
Always leave time to put things away, collect the music, re-arrange the furniture and dismiss the class in an orderly fashion.

Posture and attitude

Singing is a physical activity which requires a positive attitude and an alert posture, avoiding tension. If pupils are singing seated, briefly tell them to put their feet flat on the ground in front of them and to sit up. Hopefully you will show them by demonstrating it and an explanation will not be necessary. If standing, ask them to have their feet slightly apart and firmly on the ground, to stand up reasonably straight and to relax their shoulders.

Avoid lecturing them about posture: it will kill their enthusiasm and make them anxious. Instead, show them by example. Music should be held up so that they can see it without stooping, but without covering their faces. If they are performing without music their hands should hang loosely at their sides. Good posture does not mean standing like a row of soldiers. Encourage the pupils to respond physically to the music and feel it in their whole bodies. However, energetic swaying and clapping may be unhelpful for inexperienced singers, since it creates an unnecessary distraction and can spoil their singing. It is a good idea to work relaxation and posture exercises into your warm-up (see page 13).

Using the singing projects

The singing projects, games and exercises are arranged in a progressive order in the pack to suit pupils of all abilities and many backgrounds. However, it is recommended that you make a careful selection of material and activities to suit the different classes you teach, your own strengths and interests and your department's schemes of work. Treat the pack as a resource book of ideas and activities rather than a cure-all which can be followed slavishly from beginning to end.

Preparing material

It is important to know the songs well before you attempt to teach them. Sing them through yourself and see how all the various parts fit together. Some of the songs look complex because of the syncopated rhythms, but most can be taught very quickly once you are confident with them. Decide just how much of the material you are going to use and what your warm-up activity will be (see Part 2). A warm-up is important because it releases inhibitions, warms up the voice and focuses pupils' attention. Remember the arrangements are flexible and you should use as much as you and your class can cope with.

Preparing the room and resources

Will you work in a circle, at the piano, in groups? Will you use the computer? Will any pupils be playing instruments? Do you need other resources for follow-up activities? It is important to have the room properly arranged and equipped for the class, and that you allow time at the end for packing away, as well as finalizing assessment and homework arrangements.

Teaching the songs

Most of the songs in the pack should be taught aurally. The pupils normally see just the lyrics, and sometimes they may not even need these. Sheets of paper can be a real distraction so the more they learn by heart the better. This usually means getting the class to repeat back the song in sections after it has been sung or played to them. At this stage it is generally helpful to play the tune to them as well as singing it. Keep the music flowing and explanations to a minimum. If there are corrections you want to make, try to do it by example rather than explanation and if there are a number, wait for a convenient moment to pause and bring them to the class's attention. As soon as possible put the whole song together so they get a sense of the whole piece.

If a song is in a foreign language, go through the pronunciation of the words first of all and show pupils how to say them in the correct rhythm for the song. All pupils can learn these words if you teach them phonetically, a word or syllable at a time.

Using notation

You may sometimes want pupils to see the music as an *aide-mémoire* or to follow a harmony part – or occasionally as a sight-reading exercise.

Follow-up activities

It is important that pupils see singing as a main and integral part of their whole music education. The follow-up activities allow you to integrate singing into listening, composing, appraising and discussion work. Get them to evaluate their own work frequently and tape record their performances for this purpose.

Whole-class ensemble performance

With careful planning most songs can be combined with instruments to create impressive whole-class ensembles, with a range of instrumental parts and harmony singing. If there is time, teach everyone the song and the instrumental parts, allocating eventual performance roles near the end. Occasionally, make a real event of it by inviting a guest or performing to another class, in assembly or at a concert.

Working with larger groups

Some pieces are ideally suited to combined classes, or even an assembly-sized group. If a piece has parts, each group or class can learn a different part, to be combined at the big 'event'. Some pieces can be developed or extended for use with the whole school choir.

Harmony and part-singing

A central aim of *Singing Matters* is to encourage harmony and part-singing in the classroom. If a group can sing in unison, then harmony singing is a natural consequence. The singing projects in Part 3 use parallel parts, ostinato phrases and layered melodies to create simple but effective harmonies which can be learned aurally within a single lesson. In some songs there are more parts than would be possible for a class to tackle. In these cases, the parts are alternatives and you should choose the harmonies which you think will best suit your pupils. The full arrangement may only be possible with a choir, a large group or a particularly gifted class. *Don't feel you're expected to use all the material in a project at once: just use what suits your pupils.*

Teaching harmonies

On the whole you should teach the parts aurally. This means knowing the music well yourself before you take it to the class. You should teach it by singing and/or playing it yourself. Sometimes the harmony is created by teaching the whole class a number of separate phrases or melodies which, when allocated to groups and layered, create an 'instant harmony'.

With parallel harmonies, however, it is best to teach the main tune first and then to overlay the harmony once the main tune is running well. Often these harmonies are so natural and close to the melody that a starting note will launch the harmony part at once. Why not free yourself by using your computer to provide the accompaniment? You can then concentrate on the singing.

It is important that all the class is fully occupied and that groups are not left idle for long periods of time while others learn their parts. Encourage pupils to sing along with other parts while they are learning. If a part is difficult or groups keep merging parts, you may need to teach parts separately. This could involve teaching a group on their own before the lesson or giving the group a tape of the part and asking them to work independently, or even at home.

If a piece runs badly at first, don't give up or get irritated. It may be taking time to settle and pupils may be temporarily drawn into other parts. Keep the piece moving if possible and correct the pupils without stopping the piece if you can. Sometimes you may have to stop and re-teach the parts, but often you can intervene by briefly singing or playing along with a part. Train the class to understand non-verbal cues (gestures, nods, basic conducting) and try to keep an optimistic expression on your face! It's easy to frown if things aren't going well and the pupils will find this lack of enjoyment and confidence contagious.

It can be useful to have an instrumental player from the class doubling the parts. If you have older students, such as sixth formers, who can help, why not ask them along? Another method for a large number would be to teach individual classes different parts and then have the classes meet in an assembly or at a special event, with each group singing their part. If other staff know the songs then they can join in, perhaps leading a part.

The main harmony techniques used in this pack are as follows:

- **Echoing** Here the harmony part simply echoes the phrase sung in the melody, while the melody sustains a note. *Teach the main tune to everyone and then divide the group, cuing the second group for entry.*

- **Canon** In this a simple polyphony is created by the same melody being sung at different times by different groups. *Teach the same tune to everyone. Carefully divide the class into groups of equal strength. First divide the group into two, then gradually into further divisions.*

- **Ostinati** These are repeated short melodic phrases which can be layered or used as backings for songs. They are sometimes called **riffs**. *Always teach the first ostinato to everyone so no one is idle. Teach any further ostinati to as many people as possible. Above all, keep the pupils occupied.*

- **Heterophony** Here, a number of songs fit the same chord structure. The songs are learned separately and can then be sung against each other creating a kind of instant polyphony. *Teach the songs to everyone as separate pieces so they know them well. Then divide the group, firstly into two so that both tunes run at the same time. Then divide as far as is possible.*

- **Parallel harmonies** These are harmonies which follow the exact contours of the main melody and are therefore easy to learn. *Make sure everyone is happy with the main tune first. Select your harmonizers according to pitch of voice and ability. By giving a starting note they should manage to sing directly over the melody, especially if you support them by singing the part yourself or by playing it clearly.*

- **Single note harmonies** Here a single note harmonizes with a melody, usually following the rhythm of the tune. *It is not always easy to stay on the same note so support the harmony group by singing with them or by playing their note.*

- **Counter-melodies** These are separate tunes which complement the main melody. *These may sometimes need to be taught separately to avoid confusion with the main tune.*

Using IT and new technology

I have found the computer to be a great liberating tool in my music teaching and now use it daily in all aspects of my work. If you do not use one, I advise you to. There is nothing dehumanizing or mechanical about its effect – in fact, quite the reverse. It can do many of the more repetitive tasks in class, freeing teachers to devote their attention to the pupils. Linked to a synthesizer, computers can perform many tasks, from accompanying and multi-track recording to score-writing. Most sequencing programs are simple to use, despite sometimes daunting manuals.

Using a computer

The computer I use is a standard PC linked by MIDI to a multi-timbral synthesizer with a sequencing/score-writing program such as Steinberg Cubasis or Cubase. The sound is amplified to the class through a speaker/amplifier.

- **A multi-timbral synthesizer** is a keyboard instrument which allows you to record and layer a variety of sounds, including percussion, simultaneously. The sounds are usually realistic and of high quality.

- **A sequencing program** is the computer software which turns your computer into a multi-track recorder when linked to a synthesizer. Sequencing programs can now turn your recordings into music scores and print them out.

- **MIDI** is the cable or interface which links the PC to the synthesizer.

This set up will enable you:

i to record and play professional sounding accompaniments/backings which can be used at any volume or tempo. These can be percussion parts, piano accompaniments or full orchestrations. Once written they can be saved to disk and recalled whenever you need them
ii to provide looped ostinato backings for echo games, improvising and composing
iii to play instrumental or vocal prompts or provide parts which are missing from your class
iv to play parts to guide the singers
v to provide a steady and reliable rhythmic support to your activities.

Using other new technology

A **drum machine** can be useful for holding some music together since it is more portable than a computer. It is essential to have a variety of **portable tape-recorders**. You will need these for assessing and recording performances, group composition and improvisation work, and for teaching vocal parts to groups. If pupils perform with microphones, it is useful to be able to enhance their voices with an **effects module** which will add echo and reverb to the voice.

Accompanying the singing

The teacher

When accompanying, teachers will generally use piano, guitar or percussion. It is essential to be able to 'busk' an accompaniment from the chords/bass line of the piece. If the pupils are still learning the song, it will help to play the tune clearly over the top.

Accompaniments should be *simple*, indicating the pulse, tempo and harmonic basis, so it's best to avoid florid and attention-seeking playing. Reading a fully scored accompaniment can prevent a teacher concentrating on the class. A drum machine, or computer-sequenced drums can give the piece a 'lift'.

Busking at a keyboard instrument

An accompaniment can be busked by playing the chords of the piece to a regular rhythm or pattern. The simplest 4/4 busking pattern would interpret a chord of C thus:

When pupils are learning a song, it is helpful to play the melody. At this stage an easy busked part could consist of the melody and bass line only. At its best, busking will imply the chords of the piece and confirm the underlying rhythm, whilst playing the melody, when necessary. Many of the melodies in this book are very syncopated, so the accompaniments need to be rhythmically regular and repetitive.

Interpreting the chord symbols

The following standard chord symbols are used in *Singing Matters*:

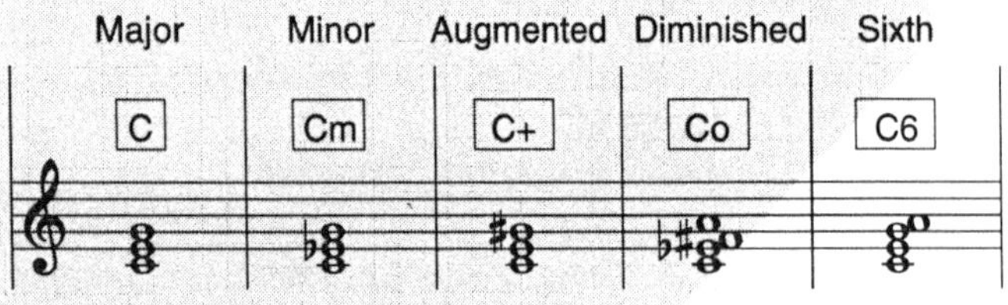

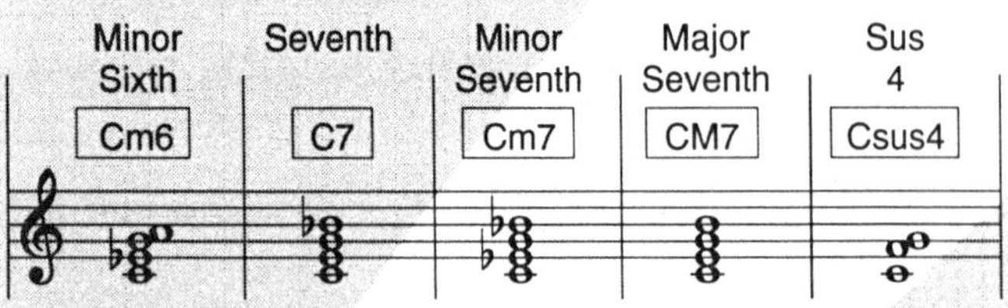

When a chord is written thus: C/G the chord of C major is played with a G in the bass. The first letter indicates the chord, the second the bass note. This is the standard way of writing inversions.

A bracketed chord or note e.g. C(7) indicates optional inclusion.

Using the busking patterns

Short examples of how an accompaniment could be busked are provided with most songs. *Note that this is a sample busking pattern for the song which must be adapted to the notes of each new chord.* Before using a song with a class, try out the busking pattern and apply it to the whole chord sequence. Play the piece through until you are confident with it.

Full accompaniments

For some songs, where the busking pattern needs to change, a full accompaniment has been provided.

What the pupils play

The singing projects in Part 3 provide opportunities for pupils to play as well as sing and instruments can be added in a variety of ways. Pupils can use keyboards, guitars, orchestral instruments and percussion to accompany the singing and double vocal parts. Although some pieces are best sung unaccompanied, some with the teacher or computer accompanying and others with just percussion, quite a few, especially the pop songs, work well if you develop a whole class instrumental version, with or without the melody.

The arrangements are flexible so that all abilities are catered for. The pupils are generally provided with a chord format, a song format, percussion and clapping parts, a busking pattern and the lyrics of the song.

The chord format

This puts the chords of the piece on to a simple grid which can be developed into differentiated instrumental parts as follows:

- **bass line:** a single-note line playing the bottom note of each chord (an easy part) or the bass line which is scored in the teacher's accompaniment (more difficult). If you have keyboards or synthesizers with good bass sounds, or a bass guitar, cello or double bass then use these for your bass part
- **single note from chord:** here, a keyboard player, instrumental player or tuned percussionist plays one note from each chord to an appropriate rhythm. The pupil will need to be told which note from the chord to play
- **two notes from chord:** here the player plays the bottom two notes of the chord
- **whole chord:** here, a keyboard player or guitarist plays the whole chord with one or two hands. Chords can be sustained, or played to a variety of ostinato rhythms
- **busked part:** keyboard players who can play with two hands can perform busked parts, as outlined earlier. A surprisingly large number of this age group can learn to busk parts and invent suitable rhythms.

The song format

This is a grid which lists the sections of the song in the order they should be performed.

Percussion and clapping parts

These are generally rhythmic ostinati. However, playing percussion to support the class's singing is not easy and the whole piece can stand or fall with the percussionists. Although the parts are repetitive, many pupils will find maintaining the pulse and tempo difficult, so choose your percussionists carefully.

When teaching the piece, mark time yourself to begin with, or use the computer or drum machine to keep everyone together. Percussionists may need to practise separately at first, joining in gradually with you or the computer beat. Clapping can add life to a piece, but it shouldn't distract from the singing.

The busking pattern

This indicates a rhythmic pattern for playing the chords and the bass line. In most cases the teacher will need to interpret it for the pupils.

Teaching the instrumental backings to the class

It is often a good idea to teach the instrumental backing to the whole class, including the ones who will eventually sing. Everyone should also learn to sing the song, once the backing is learned. Have the room arranged properly before the class comes in and hand them their part as they enter, carefully matching part to ability, so they can work on it right away (with headphones in if they are using keyboards and damped sounds if they are using tuned percussion).

Once they know their way round the music, call everything to a halt and work your way through the whole song in small sections, with all the class playing at once. Use the drum machine/computer to keep the pulse and lead them through the piece by numbering each chord or beat and counting through each line of the music. The number will correspond to the note they play.

Begin slowly, gradually speed up, increasing the amount of the song they play each time until the whole song is learned. At this stage the melody can be played over the top and hopefully the class will be keen to sing it. Always count into each section you are rehearsing and clearly state which notes of which line you are going to play. Only allow the headphones out of keyboards when it's nearly ready.

Games and warm-ups

Singing Matters contains a wider range of games and warm-ups than you will need for a single group. Every class is different, so you need to select an activity which suits you, the class and their needs.

The games often produce much noise and excitement, so you should establish clear codes of behaviour with the class before attempting them. Some games ask pupils to do strange and seemingly 'silly' things, but these activities should be presented with all the discipline and gravitas of any serious musical activity. After all, they are serious. They will loosen inhibitions, warm up the whole range of the voice and develop group sensitivity. However, some games are funny and will set everyone off laughing. Wonderful! There is no better warm-up for singing than genuine laughter.

Keep the pace of the lesson moving and use the games as warm-ups to a main activity. Afterwards explain the purpose of the game and point out to the class how it helped their singing. You are certain to find their singing does improve as a result.

The more you do such games with groups, the greater your confidence with delivering them will become. It might be best to try some out with a small and motivated group first, to give you practice and to see the effect they have on the pupils. Groups who are new to the school are also good to practise on, since they are usually prepared to accept any activity as legitimate in their first weeks. Once used to such activities they will see them as the norm and enjoy them.

Discuss these activities with a drama colleague who may be able to help you with the delivery of voice games and who could perhaps incorporate them into drama lessons.

Imitation/mirroring technique

Here the class copy everything you do as you do it, paying attention to pulse, tempo, pitch and dynamics. This technique encourages the class to:

- focus on you as group leader
- watch and listen with sensitivity
- learn something without lengthy explanation
- combine rhythm with vocal work
- combine sound and movement.

First mirroring/imitation activities

It works well if pupils are arranged in a circle for these activities.

Ask the class to copy your clapping exactly. Change the speed, leave gaps, stop, start, clap and repeat rhythmic patterns; alter the dynamics, clap with your whole hand or just finger-tips. Encourage the class to do this swiftly and exactly. Praise them extensively for any sensitive copying. Return to this game frequently, extending it in the following ways:

- Increase the range of things you do for them to copy: incorporate knees, feet, posture, standing, sitting, moving at different speeds and a variety of movements and gestures. Repeat the gestures until the whole class are with you.

- Combine movement with sound. Once the class copy gestures well, make vocal sounds to go with them. For example:
  - swooping downward movements of the hand with *Sssh* noises
  - prodding the air with index fingers, making high pitched *boop, boop, boop* noises, altering the pitch of the note with the height of your hands
  - wide gestures with long expressions of delight
  - sudden forward air punches combined with the word *Hey*! Alter the force of the punch with the volume of the word, and the pitch with its height
  - graceful movements combined with all sorts of slow contented sighs, once again passing from high to low
  - hands on the hips, rocking laughter
  - opening out hands suddenly to *tsaa* noises
  - moving hands on a straight plane backwards and forwards to make a continuous pitched *humm*.

Pupils can subsequently work in pairs, taking it in turns to lead in sound and movement. Reward and praise whenever you can.

Imitation exercises with specific purposes

These mirroring exercises can also work well in pairs once they have been demonstrated by you.

Body relaxation

i Stretch right up as high as you can, looking up. Gradually unfold from the top, first by letting your wrist flop, then your elbow, then your shoulder, then your neck. Finally flop downwards from the waist, and have a shake-out and groan at the bottom.

ii Reach up high, and look up. Then, folding at the waist, fall forwards making a huge descending sigh as you go, from very high to very low. Remain down for a while shaking out and groaning.

iii Repeatedly raise and lower the shoulders first together, then individually. Rotate them forwards and backwards, together and individually. Smoothly rotate the head, stretching the neck fully forwards, back and to the sides.

Posture

i If seated, move your feet forwards, keeping them flat on the ground and sit up with your back straight.

ii If standing, stretch your arms out in front of you and then raise your arms, still outstretched, above your head. Then lower your arms, leaving your chest raised. Stand with feet slightly apart, well balanced and springy.

Jaw and face

i Tighten jaw and drop jaw alternately, then make a huge noisy yawn with your mouth open.

ii Exaggeratedly chew imaginary gum with full teenage attitude, letting it get stuck on back teeth, obliging you to remove it with your tongue.

iii Make mad, wild facial expressions.

iv Chant an athletic vocal phrase like: *The lips, the teeth, the tip of the tongue*, or *Peter Piper picked a peck of pickled pepper.*

v Let your jaw hang loose, clench your fists and shake them vigorously up and down. Your jaw should wobble freely.

Diaphragm

i Get the class to breathe in and out slowly in sync with you, observing how you fill your lungs without raising your shoulders.

ii Breathe in to a count of 4, hold for 4 and breathe out for 4. This can be increased to 8 or 16. To strengthen the exhalation, breathe out to a long *Sssssssss*.

iii Blow out an imaginary candle, using your forefinger as the candle.

iv Whistle a tune or exhale slowly to the sound *Vvvv* or *Zzzz*.

v Repeat a word forcefully like, *Yes!* or *Go!* or *Hey!*

vi Laugh exaggeratedly.

vii Laugh silently, making all the body movements but with no noise, not even a whisper.

Vocal range and tone

i Move your hands or whole body up and down, altering the pitch of your chosen sound as you move. Make the type of sound match the gesture you make and vary from sharp staccato sounds with stabbing gestures, to smooth sounds with soft caressing movements.

ii Sing a continuous note to the sound *-ing* (the *g* is silent as in 'sing' – this is a nasal hum). Explore the whole vocal range, going from your highest to lowest note in the manner of a gentle siren. Guide the pitch with hand movements which the pupils can copy. A roomful of sirens will emerge.

iii Intone a melody to the sound *-ng*, for example *Amazing grace* (see page 166).

iv *Yeow* like an angry cat throughout your vocal range.

v Lead a wild, stationary, car race with driving actions, car noises, screeching breaks and gear changes.

vi Get the group to crouch then, following you, to bounce up and down to the revving sound of a motorbike: *Mmm, Mmm*, then you launch into the air with the class following and shout, *Motorbike!* with your arms pointing upwards.

Pitch

i Sing a note within the range of the whole class (middle C) with your outstretched hand at a fixed central point. They join you on this note. Move slowly up and down, step-wise, moving your hand up and down as you do. The class follow both the pitches and the hand movements.

ii This game can equally well be played in pairs. As an extension activity, partner B must first sing A's note and then think of a new note for A to sing.

iii Sing short phrases to the group, which they must join in with. This can be well achieved over some of the ostinato backings provided (see page 25).

More games

Many of the following games are best achieved in a circle, although teachers should arrange the group in a manner appropriate to their circumstances.

1 Vocal ice-breaker

Ask everyone to see the word *H-E-Y!* in their mind and to say it together after 4. Next they should try to attract the attention of someone on the other side of the room, so they need to raise their voices, again after 4.

Now they are on the football field and they need to get someone's attention urgently who's a long way away. They really need to shout that *Hey!* after 4.

Divide the circle in half. Group A shout *Hey!* on beats 1 and 3 of a 4-beat bar and Group B on beats 2 and 4. Which side does it the loudest? Now divide the circle into four. Each sub-group gets one beat of the 4-beat bar on which to shout *Hey!* Speed up the beat slightly. Which of the four groups is best?

As extension work you can:

- include a secretive, whispered *Hey!*
- include a long swooping *Hey!*, which could imply impatience
- say the word *Hey* to a variety of moods, including delight, surprise, shock
- add the sounds, *Helooo, Ouch, Ho, Hee, Yahoo!* for variety
- ask each of the four sub-groups to present their expletive in a different manner, including two *Hey!*s per beat (as quavers).

2 Vocal ice-breaker

For this game tribal chanting sounds are chosen, unpitched. For example:

- *Hooh!* (a grunt) *Hah!* (a frightening sound)
- *Hey-ah!* (a loud shout)
- *Hey!* (an abrupt shout)
- *Hotcha!* (percussive and aggressive)

After everyone has practised them with you, divide the pupils in the circle into four groups, A, B, C, D, and allocate a sound to each. The sounds can occur on particular beats as follows, so that the vocal sounds are layered:

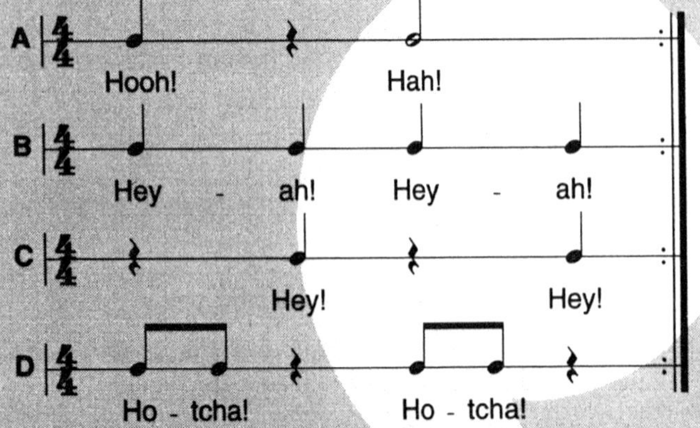

On a given cue the chants are moved round the circle, so B pick up A's sounds and C pick up B's etc. This obliges them to listen to what others are doing. Which group made the best sounds? Which made the best changes? This activity can be combined with drumming, clapping or on-the-spot rhythmic walking.

3 Counting and chanting

In these activities beats of the bar are replaced by vocal sounds. First, ask the class to clap all together a steady 4-beat phrase. Whilst they are clapping ask them to substitute a particular beat by a vocal sound, *Hey! Ho!* or another interjection. Keep changing the chosen beat. Stop them clapping occasionally and replace each clapped beat with a short panted breath, so patterns like the following emerge:

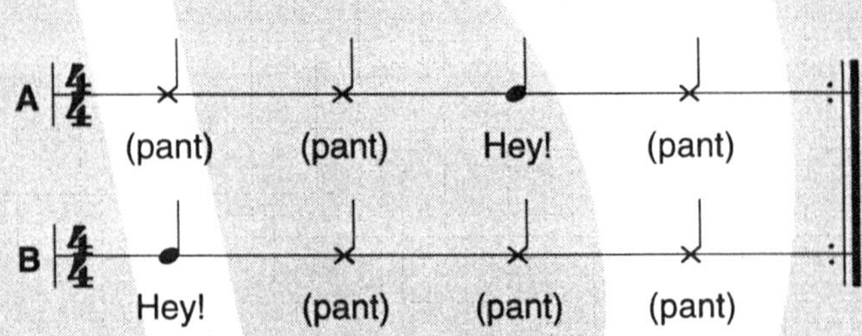

Now divide the group into three. Group A group their beats in 2s, Group B in 3s and Group C in 4s. Each group shouts *Hey!* on the first beat of their grouping, whilst clapping the other beats, and all groups share the same pulse. Mark time with a loud percussion instrument to keep everyone together and bring all the groups in together after a 4-beat count-in. Everyone will shout on the first beat and occasionally all the *Hey!*s will coincide. Which group holds their rhythm together best?

4 Fun with pitch

Face the group with your outstretched hands pointing towards each other, fingertip to fingertip. When your hands meet this represents your starting note (middle C). Keep your left hand stationary and move your right hand up and down to indicate movement up and down in pitch. The class should be humming a C at the start and sliding freely up and down in response to your hand movements. You can really have fun with the group, moving your hand slowly and quickly.

5 Gentle exercises for breath, pitch and diaphragm

Try these yourself first and then incorporate them into a warm-up activity:

i With your right arm outstretched by your side, inhale slowly as you move your arm in an arc to be level with your head. Exhale slowly by gently moving your arm back to its original position. You can also hum a note as you exhale.

ii With your right arm outstretched by your side, inhale slowly as you move your arm in an arc to be level with your head. Exhale by making your right hand imitate a paint aerosol can and spray-paint your name on to an imaginary wall in front of you, whilst making the sound *Sssssss* to represent the sound of the aerosol. This must be achieved in a single breath. You can also draw your house, an imaginary horizon, or, indeed, any picture.

iii Inhale in the same way. This time on exhalation draw a picture of an imaginary horizon, or a face, or mountain scene. Instead of hissing, hum a note, which rises when your hand goes up and drops as your hand does. Other vocal sounds can represent features in your picture.

6 Group hum

This is a simple activity where everyone in the class hums any note at a given signal, but must maintain pitch. Another signal indicates a change to a second note, after which they return to their first. Class members can breathe when necessary, as long as they resume their note.

Next, pupils pick up the note of a partner, so they both sing the same. This pair pick up the note from another pair so four share a note. This can go on until there are just two notes – or even one in the room.

7 Voice tennis

Here a sound is sent by one of a pair to a partner who is some distance away. The sound can be as weird or inventive as the 'server' likes and the respondent must send it back in as close an imitation as possible. As soon as it is sent back the server must think of an entirely different, contrasting sound. Each partner has four turns to serve. Points are lost if the sound is not returned exactly or the server fails to think of a sufficiently contrasting sound. Scoring is as for tennis. If students are grouped in threes then they can take turns in scoring. Prepare this activity by challenging an individual in the class yourself, demonstrating all the range of sounds that can be made while a student scores.

8 Sound orchestra

Divide the class into groups or pairs of vocal sounds. For example there can be orchestral sections making brass, woodwind, string or percussion sounds, a group singing a song, a grunting group, a hissing group, a panting group, a humming group, a rhythm group, a siren group, a farmyard group, a sobbing group, a laughing group, a sighing group etc. Ask them to make their sounds:

- all at once with varying dynamics indicated by yourself
- cumulatively with groups entering as you point to them
- with a student conductor indicating when groups should perform and at what dynamic level.

9 Responding vocally to hand gestures

The leader, who can be the teacher or a pupil, makes imaginative hand gestures to which the whole group responds vocally. These can be shapes and movements of varying sizes and speeds. The same game can be undertaken in pairs and linked to the 'mirror' games – see pages 12-13).

10 Responding vocally to graphic stimuli

A series of varied and imaginative graphic symbols are displayed on a board. The teacher points to one and asks the class or an individual to make an appropriate vocal sound for the chosen symbol. This can be made into a competition between two halves of the class, where points are awarded for the appropriateness of the sound to the symbol. Always demonstrate this activity yourself first.

11 Vocal machine soundscape

The teacher begins by repeating a rhythmic ostinato which sounds mechanical. Then pupils are invited to contribute new and different sounds to this classroom machine. They contribute when and if they feel they have something to offer. Pupils must complement each other's sounds, choosing different rhythms, contrasting pitches and tempi and different types of sound. There is scope for hissing, clanking, booing, low hums, sirens, whistles, ticking and banging. Discuss the possible range of sounds before you start.

12 Jungle soundscape

What sort of sounds do we hear in a jungle? Monkeys, tigers, snakes, the wind, the rain, a waterfall, a distant tribe, bird cries etc. Using vocal sounds or a combination of percussion and voices, invite the class to contribute sounds to the jungle soundscape. Pupils can work in pairs or small groups to contribute different types of sounds. Soundscapes can be created for a variety of scenes including a haunted house, a city street, a crowded beach or a football match.

13 Layering unpitched vocal ostinati and words

The following are examples of layered ostinato patterns using rhythm and speech. They can be combined with, or spring from percussion work. Pupils can compose similar layered ostinati themselves.

Divide the group into halves, three, four or five as required, so you can layer sounds, rhythms and words with each group taking a particular vocal ostinato. Teach the whole class each ostinato so that you can pass the ostinati round the circle at a given cue. Groups will pick up the one from the group on their left.

1 Boom! Ooh! Yatatata!

Note: The 'Ooh' lasts a little longer than a crotchet, is pitched high initially but trails a little lower as it is held. Hundreds of songs can be sung over this humorous backing including The grand old Duke of York, Yankee Doodle, My old man, When you're smiling *and many more.*

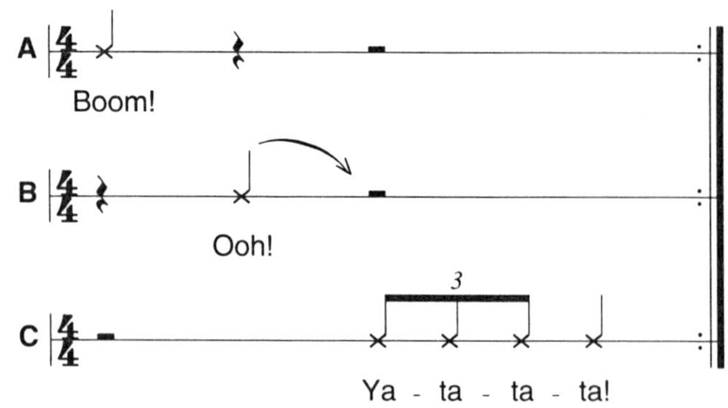

2 Rock beats

Note: These can spring from work with hand-held percussion. Use the voice to mimic the percussion instruments shown.

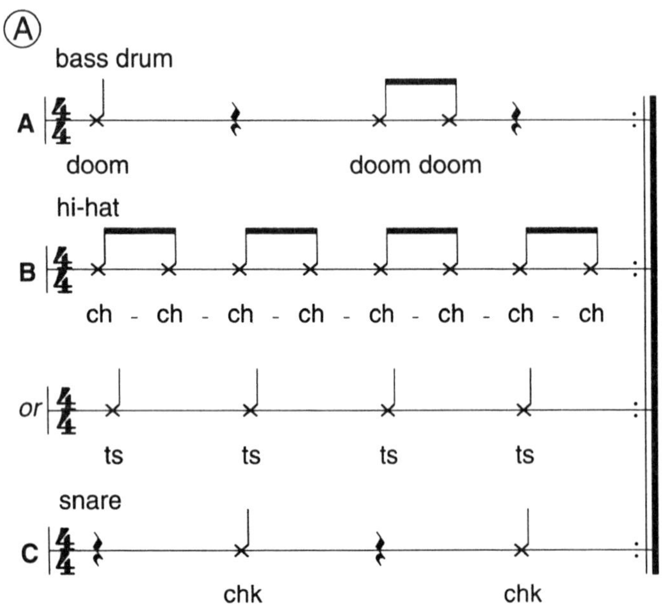

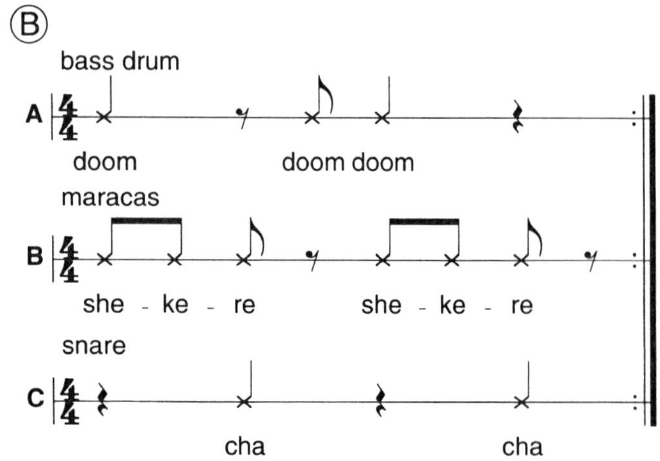

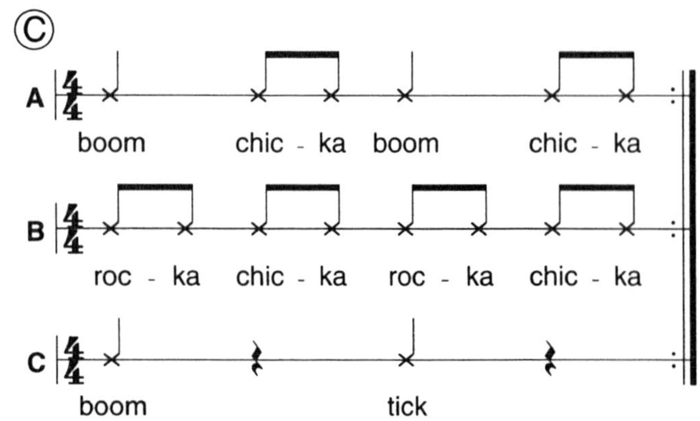

3 Rap rhythm

Note: This can be the backing for a rap. Many pupils seem to know Wannabe *by the Spice Girls, which will fit.*

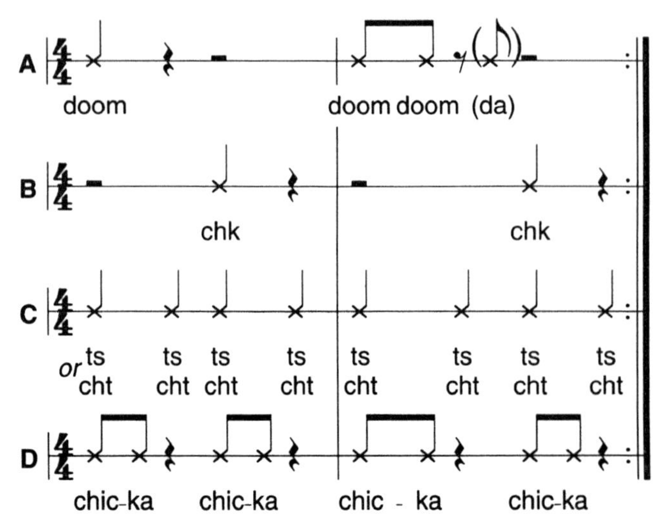

4 Latin rhythm

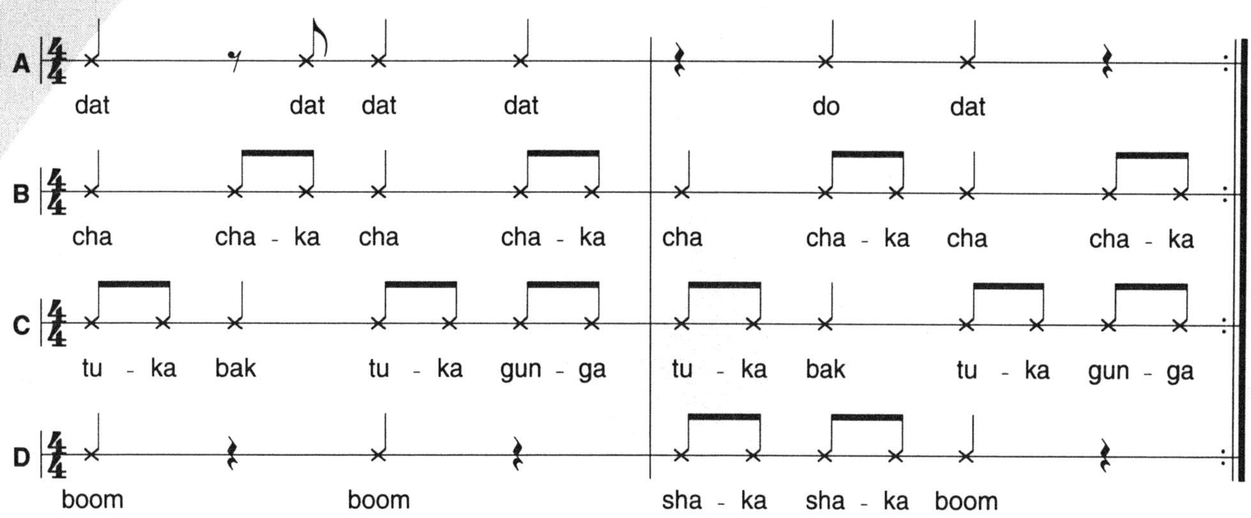

5 Boom! Shake!

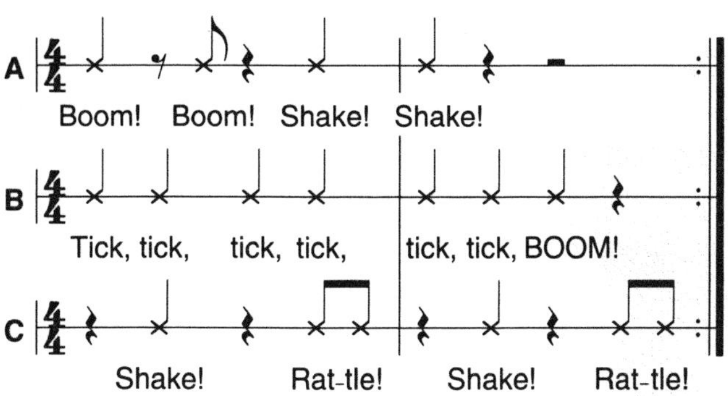

6 Train departure

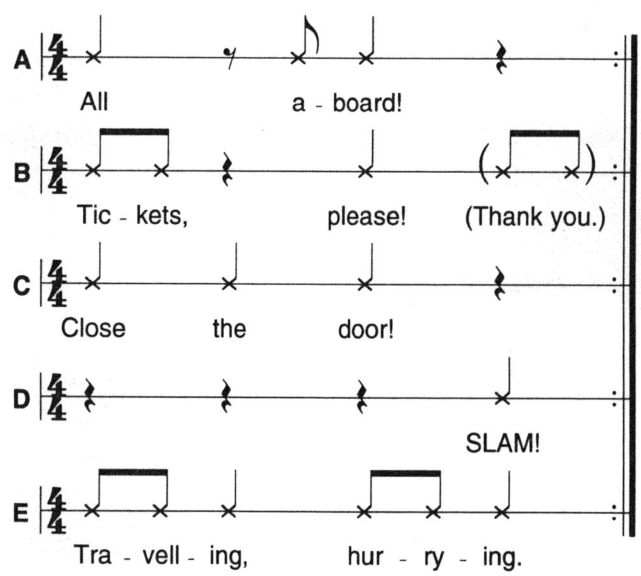

7 Classroom

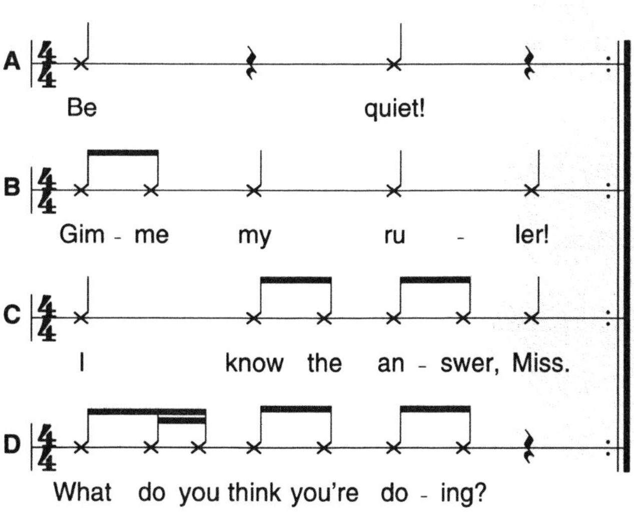

Note: All of these rhythms can be transferred to percussion instruments. Pupils can make up their own ostinato pieces in a particular setting, using words and phrases they would hear in that place.

14 Layering pitched ostinati

The ostinati here are taught in precisely the same way as in game 13. It is useful to start these activities with a collective 'hum' to establish the keynote. Once again the ostinati can be passed round the circle. Chords, a drone, percussion and clapping can help, if they are too difficult to sustain unaccompanied.

1 Move on over

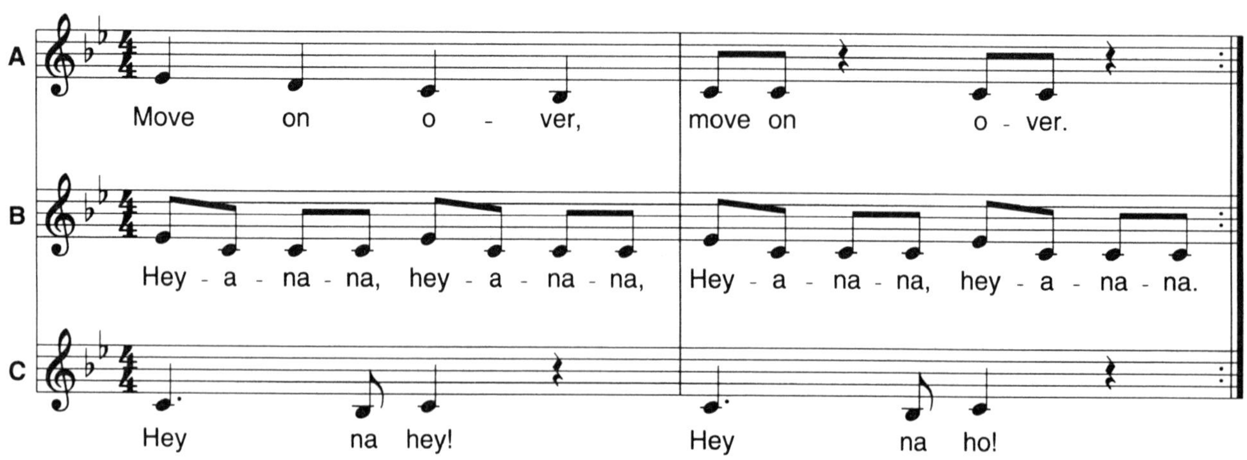

Note: This can be enhanced with quaver beat drumming and a drone on C.

2 Freedom highway

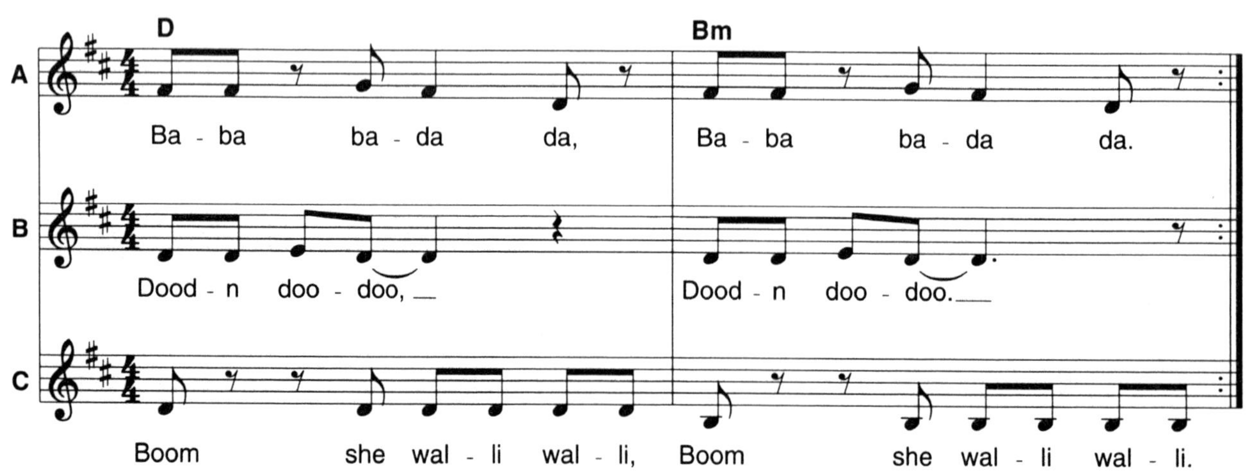

Note: This can be enhanced with off-beat clapping. This ostinato is used as the basis for a song on page 146.

3 Na, na-na na-na

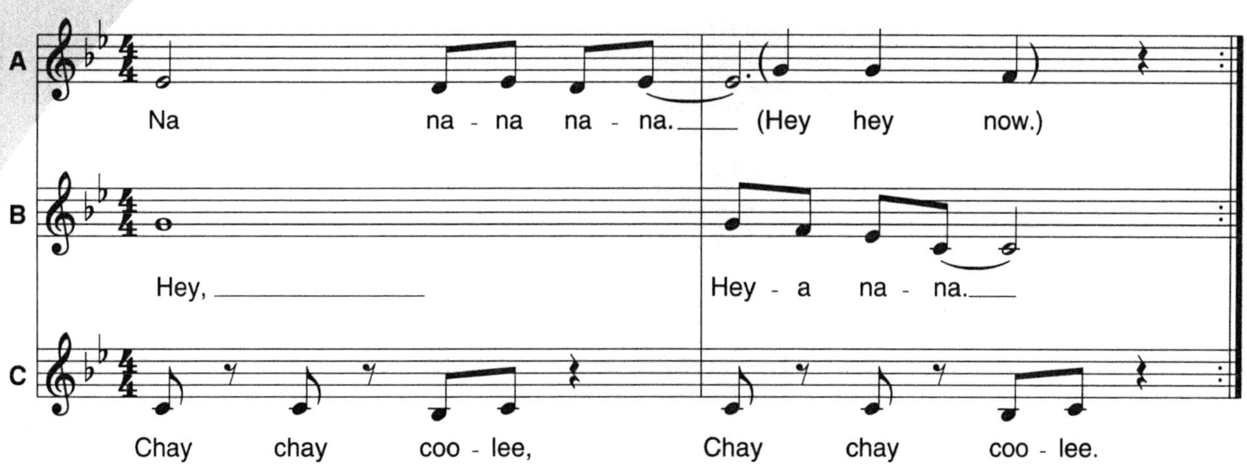

Note: off-beat clapping or a rock beat will help this piece.

4 Gimme some more

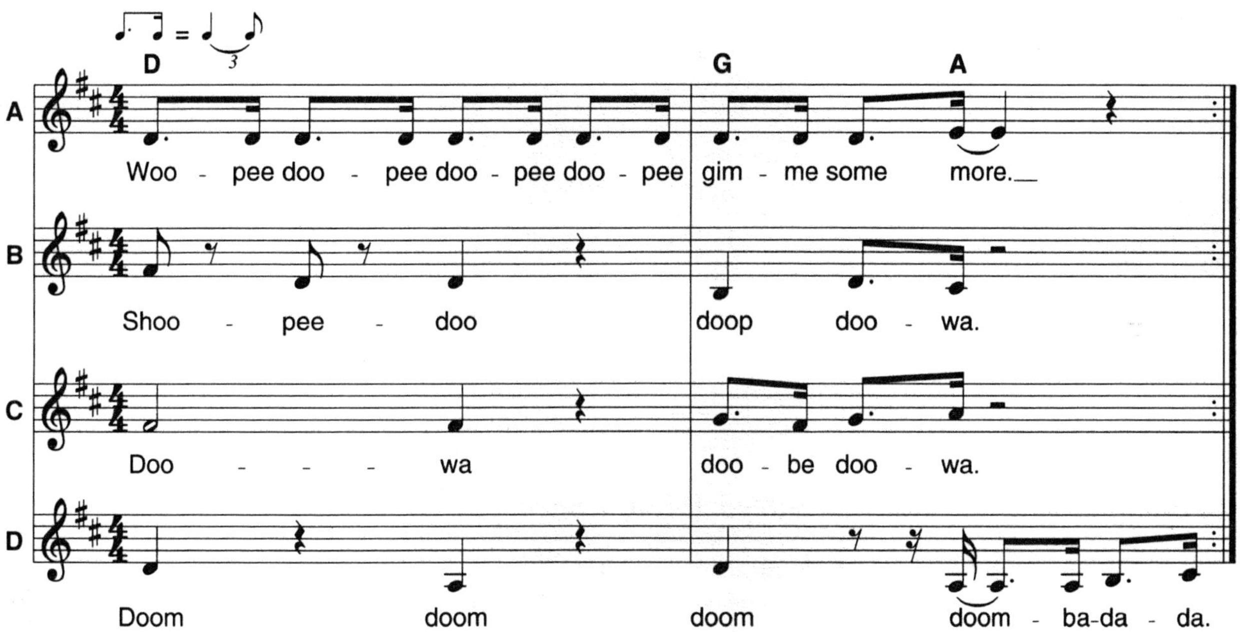

Teacher-led vocal exercises

The following teacher-led vocal exercises are designed to develop tone and vocal control. They are best done with the class grouped as they would be for class singing. The object of the activities is to prepare the voice for singing so they should not be regarded as an end in themselves. Approach them in a spirit of fun and do invent your own on this basis.

Exercise 1

Aim: To prepare the voice for singing through an arpeggio and vowel exercise

i Sing the phrase as written.
ii Shift the piece to lower then higher keys, moving by tones or semitones.
iii Change the manner of singing to: *staccato, legato, glissando.*
iv Change the two vowels to :
eeh-oh
aah-ooh
aw-ah
Try to make the class sing pure vowels rather than dipthongs.
v Other variations could include: *Hip-hip; Yang, yang; Kee, kah; Na-nee; La-lee.*

Olay

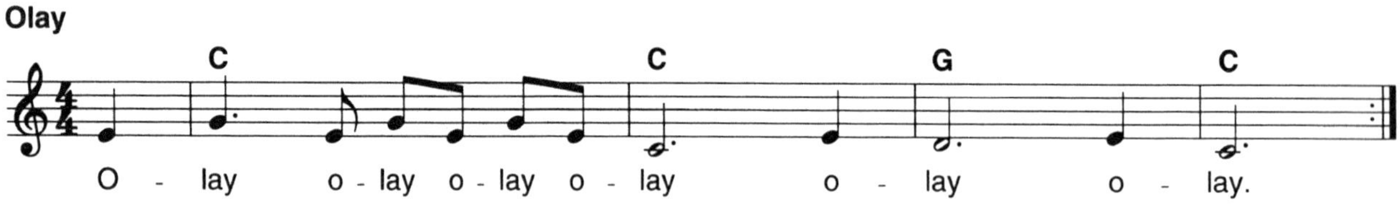

Exercise 2

Aim: To energize singing across an octave, through an exuberant and well-known phrase

i Sing the phrase in the original key to get energetic singing.
ii Move the phrase up in semitones, if possible, to extend the range.

Hallelujah!

Exercise 3

Aim: To achieve sustained singing and longer breaths, using sounds similar to those in Exercise 2

i After exercises to aid breathing (page 13), first sing this phrase *legato* in two breaths, and eventually in a single breath. Aim at pure vowels and avoid dipthongs.
ii Transpose the phrase up and down by tones and semitones.
iii To practise long notes, extend each note of the exercise to a minim or semibreve.

Alleluia

Exercise 4

Aim: To exercise the diaphragm as a warm-up for singing

i Sing the phrase to *Hip* with energy.
ii Replace *Hip* with *Yes, Ha, Ho* and *Hee.*
iii Transpose the phrase upwards by semitones.
iv Now sing the phrase *legato* to a single vowel, *Ooh, Aah*, etc.

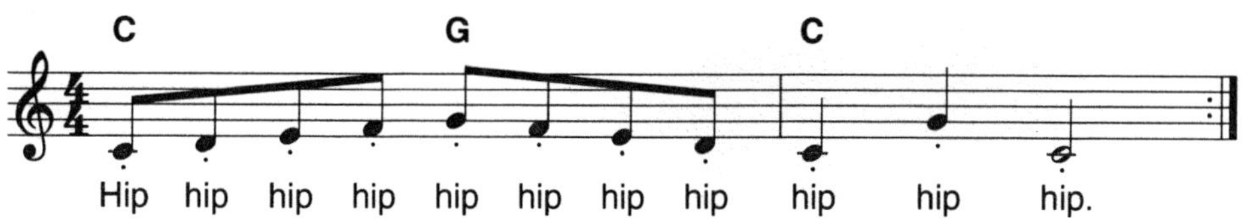

Exercise 5

Aim: To warm the voice and exercise the jaws with a downward phrase

i Sing the phrase as written, then transpose up by semitones.
ii Substitute *Yah* with *Lah, Tah, Kah, Fah, Bah.*
iii Sing the phrase to a single vowel, *legato: Aah, Ooh, Eeh.*

Exercise 6

Aim: To help articulation by repeating phrases up and down the scale

i Sing the phrase with energy.
ii Use other nonsense words: *bogabilla, Peter Piper, Hillaholla, Manatuba* – or people's names.

Exercise 7

Aim: To sing a range of notes *glissando* before singing them separately

i Sing the phrase as written.
ii Move to nearby keys and substitute other vowels.

Exercise 8

Aim: To warm the voice across an octave and to rehearse various consonant sounds

i Sing the phrase as written, and then in nearby keys.
ii Substitute *Bumble bee* with *Tumble tee, Kumble kee, Fumble fee,* etc.

Bumble bee

Exercise 9

Aim: To develop flexibility in tone and manner of singing through aural imitation

The following simple accompaniment runs throughout – except in the section where the phrase is to be sung like a monk, where it changes to C minor.

Over this the teacher sings each phrase, which is immediately repeated by the class. This call and response should happen at least twice on each numbered section. The phrase not only develops and changes, but the *manner* of singing also alters. The teacher and class will sing as an opera singer, as monks, whispering and with an American accent. Add to this any variations you can think of.

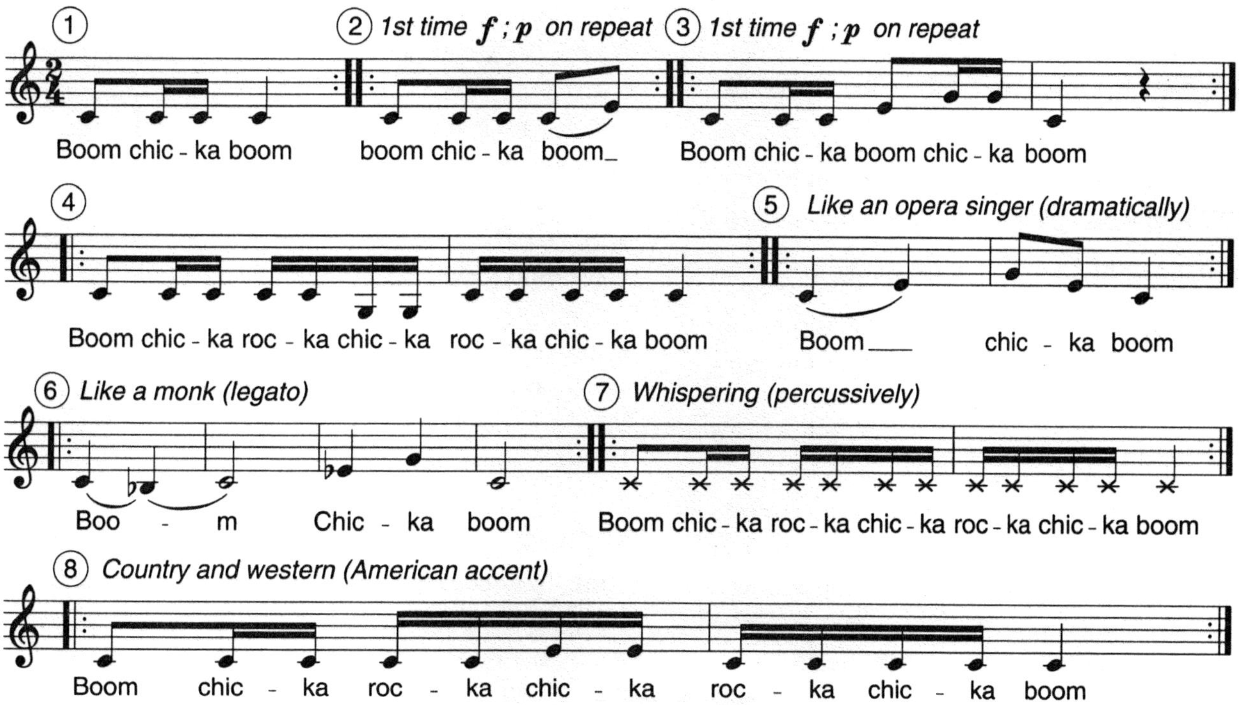

Games for larger spaces

These games use peer pressure and competition to encourage singing and they require adequate space and careful planning. Use a hall, large classroom or drama studio and clear the furniture to the sides of the room. They may not suit all classes, and may be best done in a drama lesson.

Game 1

Aim: To encourage singing through teamwork and competition

Pupils should stand in their own space, away from others.

i Pupils are asked to think of a song they know and to inwardly sing it through. It can be a song with words or a famous tune sung to *La*.

ii They move into pairs and teach each other their songs. This will be noisy – hopefully! They must decide on one of these songs as their chosen piece.

iii Still in pairs, they rehearse their song together.

iv Each pair meets another pair and each must sing their song to the other pair. This group of four must decide which of the two songs they will sing.

v Each group of four must rehearse its song.

vi Each group of four meets another group of four. Each must perform and once again a song is chosen for all eight to sing.

vii Each group of eight must rehearse its song.

viii Groups of eight now face each other in a circle and, when instructed, perform to each other. If they still seem shy get them all to sing at once, whatever the noise. Encourage them to clap and move their bodies when they sing.

What happens next depends on the size of the class. Either there are two or more groups who will all know different songs – or the whole thing can be taken further, to the point where the whole class is singing the same song. If there are several groups, a competition for the strongest, clearest, most tuneful performance can follow.

Game 2

Aim: To overcome vocal inhibitions

The class is divided into two teams in a room cleared of furniture and obstacles. Team A forms a blocking line across the middle of the room, while Team B is positioned in two halves, one at each end of the room, either side of Team A. One half of Team B must send a musical message to the other half. The message is specified by you on paper and could be a particular melody or a range of sounds.

Meanwhile Team A has to try and block the message. They, too, will have specific instructions as to the range of blocking sounds they can use. They could also sing specified melodies or use specified sounds from the 'sound orchestra' activity (see page 15). People in Team A can be doing different things, whereas those in Team B are all sending the same message.

The competitive team element forces the pupils to do everything at the top of their voices so as not to let the group down. Above all they cannot shout on either team and should be disqualified if they do. Impose very strict time limits and give each team equal turns at sending and blocking musical messages. Then count up how many messages get across and decide on a winning team.

Timid groups who won't make a noise can turn into noisy savages in this game so don't let it get out of hand and be very strict! Avoid using it frequently or for long periods as some pupils may strain their voices.

Game 3

Aim: To encourage teamwork and to overcome inhibitions

A number of song titles (no more than four in total) are written on small pieces of paper, one title per sheet. Each pupil is handed a title. If necessary teach the melodies (which can be well-known tunes as well as songs) before beginning the activity. The melodies can be suggested by the pupils. Since there is a competitive element it is worth establishing ground rules of behaviour beforehand and clarifying the signal which will indicate silence.

i Ask the pupils to stand to the edge of the room and all at once to start singing their melodies whilst moving around the room. The object is for each singer to find and link up with other people singing the same song. The first group to link up, and continue singing, wins.

ii Once the groups are established a further competitive element can be added – which group sings loudest, which sings most clearly, which sings most tunefully?

Game 4

Aim: To sing with confidence in friendly competition

i In pairs pupils agree on a song and rehearse it.

ii Pupil A of the pair is then either blindfolded, or works with eyes closed. Each pupil B must then move to the other end of the room.

iii At a signal from the teacher all the Bs start singing their tunes as a signal to their partner. At the teacher's instruction all the As make their way slowly across the room to find their partner, locating them by the melody. Pupils are disqualified for looking, or for bumping into other pupils. The first six partners to reunite win.

Singing, improvising and composing over looped backings

For these activities you will need to play and record the provided backings into a computer sequencing program such as Cubase or Cubasis, driving a multi-timbral synthesizer. Put the sequencer on 'cycle' and it will continually repeat. Save the backing to disk and recall it whenever you need it.

Backing A (Dorian mode)

The piece on the following page works as a drone backing in the Dorian mode and can form the basis for simple ostinato singing layers as well as composition and improvisation work for both voice and instruments. Note that the harp part needs to be relatively quieter than the other parts so it does not intrude on the singing activities.

Teaching the ostinato melodies

The four ostinato melodies can be sung over the backing singly or in layers but this activity works equally well with voices and instruments.

i Try teaching this aurally as a keyboard piece first, by singing the letter names of the ostinato melodies to the class. Tune 1 needs to be taught cumulatively, starting with just D F D D.

ii Once the pupils can play the tunes, ask them to say the names of the letters as they play them. Inevitably they sing the phrases, often with great enthusiasm. The lesson then becomes a singing lesson.

iii The ostinato melodies layer on top of each other so, once the tunes are learned, the class can be divided into halves and then quarters with each group singing one of the tunes over the drone backing. Pupils can sing or sing and play the melodies.

iv The rounds *Hey, ho, nobody home* (see page 153) and the *Canoe round* (see page 151) also fit on to this backing.

Improvising and composing over the backing

i Invent 2-bar phrases for the pupils to repeat by singing or playing, call and response fashion. Keep repeating them until they get them right. It's best to play and sing at the same time.

ii Ask the pupils to invent 2-bar phrases in the same manner. They can also play and sing their melodies.

iii Once they have invented their phrases, get them to teach their tune to a partner or to present it to the class. For the moment, the tune will be to *'la'* or the note names.

Follow-up work

i Pupils can build 4-bar phrases and then construct whole songs on the format A, A1, BA with A and B as 4-bar melodic phrases.

ii Pupils can be given words for a song and asked to see if they can write a tune for it over the backing.

iii Give the pupils the first half of a melodic phrase and ask them to compose the second half.

Instrumental parts

Note: The harp part should be quieter than the others. The piano part is an alternative to the harp. The 'light' part is a very quiet ambient part using a very warm, unobtrusive ensemble string sound. The most important parts are the bass and drums.

Ostinato melodies (to be sung or played over the backing)

Backing B (Pentatonic)

This is a pentatonic backing using the notes D, E, G, A, B with E as the tonic, well suited to call and response singing, melodic invention and improvising. Similar activities to those used for Backing A can be employed.

Instrumental parts

Note: The koto and xylophone parts should be unobtrusive.

Backing C (I–VI–IV–V)

This backing for melody writing and improvisation links to Project 20 on page 97. It can work for singing, playing or a combination of the two. Keep repeating the following activities until the pupils are confident with them:

i Begin by asking pupils to sing the bass line in their own octave.
ii Next ask them to sing any note which harmonizes.
iii Now ask them to move more freely, two notes per chord.
iv Finally ask them to invent a tune over the top at their own speed.

1 Project Three popular chants

Source

The songs in this project are three chants, well known to most young people, which can be sung separately and simultaneously to create instant part-singing.

A *Olay (Under pressure)* A football chant, sung all over the UK and Eire which many pupils will already sing for fun. It is also an excellent arpeggio exercise, and features in the vocal exercises on page 20.

B *Ging gang guli* Another arpeggio-based chant, made famous by the Scout and Guide movement.

C *A ram sam sam* This chant is also popular in many convivial contexts and is allegedly of Moroccan origin.

Singing style

As long as the pupils are in tune, try to harness the spirit of the football terraces. 'Guli' is pronounced with a long 'goo-'. The pieces can work well unaccompanied, but the simple chordal accompaniment will really help their singing. Use the melodies to practise different ways of singing: *legato, staccato, forte, piano*, dramatically, timidly.

Teaching the songs

The pupils will pick these up easily and sing them with great gusto. Teach the songs individually to the whole class, so they feel secure with all three and encourage them to sing loudly. Divide the class in half and get one half to sing *Olay* while the other half sings *Ging gang guli*. It should sound terrific, but make sure you get the tempo right. To make them work together, *Olay* has to run a little faster than usual and *Ging gang* a little slower. A speed of ♩ = 120 is recommended. Next mix in *A ram sam sam*. Try it as a pair with either of the others, and then try to put all three together! To maintain interest and momentum the groups should take turns to sing each tune.

Follow-up work

1 Try to create a football terrace choir with the three songs running simultaneously. With hand gestures instruct the groups to sing louder and softer so that the tunes stand out in turn.

2 Have a competition. Which group sings clearest/loudest/most in tune? What other sports chants do the pupils know? Get class members to teach the class their favourite chants and team anthems. Pupils could discuss why these chants are important and what the pleasures are in singing them.

1 Project
Three popular chants

arr. Patrick Allen

2 Project Wonderwall

Source

Composed by Noel Gallagher of the pop group Oasis, the song in this project is already a classic (to the extent of being parodied in Mike Flowers' version). It appears on their album (*What's the story) Morning Glory?*

Singing style

Most pupils of this age know the song well. For this project it has been transposed to fit the range of the whole class. Changed voices will usually sing it an octave lower. Classes sing this well, finding the syncopations easy and fitting the words neatly into the semiquavers. Make sure they hold on the long notes of the chorus and practise this separately. Note that there is more echo at the end here than there is on the original recording.

Teaching the song

Classes should launch into this easily and should be able to run through it approximately first time. If you don't know the song well, find a recording to hear how it should go, because you'll come unstuck relying too heavily on the notation. Go over the details of the words, focusing on how they fit the melody – some members of the class may be expert on this. If you are working on a detail there is no need for accompaniment, but the song works best with piano or guitar and drums, or you could programme a backing into the computer.

Accompanying the song

When teaching the melody play it with the bass line. However, once pupils have learnt the tune use the busking pattern to accompany them. The drum part can be given to class members or programmed into the computer. A class accompaniment could consist of:

i easy bass part, made from the bottom note of the chords
ii chord part, playing on each crotchet or syncopated (see busking patterns on page 33)
iii two-handed keyboard part based on busking pattern
iv percussion
v pupil reading the piano bass
vi pupil playing a single note from each chord on each crotchet.

Follow-up work

1 Oasis have been one of the most successful and controversial bands of the 1990s. What do pupils think are the appeals of their music? Focus on appealing chord sequences, singable melodies and an acoustic/electric sound. Will they last as long as the Beatles?

2 'Britpop' is a phenomenon of the 1960s and 1990s. Who are and were the influential British artists? How does their style differ from American pop? Focus on the regional pop of the British Isles and notice its differences; for example, Madness from London, Runrig from Scotland, the Cranberries from Ireland. There are a number of groups who sing in the Celtic languages.

2 Project Wonderwall

Noel Gallagher arr. Patrick Allen

2 Project Wonderwall

2 Project

Wonderwall

Pupil's sheet

Noel Gallagher arr. Patrick Allen

Verse

1 Today is gonna be the day
That they're gonna throw it back to you.
By now you should've somehow
Realized what you got to do.
I don't believe that anybody
Feels the way I do about you now.

2 Backbeat, the word is on the street
That the fire in your heart is out.
I'm sure you've heard it all before
But you never really had a doubt.
I don't believe that anybody
Feels the way I do about you now.

Middle 1

And all the roads we have to walk are winding
And all the lights that lead us there are blinding.
There are many things that I would
Like to say to you – but I don't know how —

Chorus

Because maybe, you're gonna be the one
who saves me?
And after all – you're my Wonderwall.

3 Today was gonna be the day?
But they'll never throw it back to you.
By now you should've somehow
Realized what you're not to do.
I don't believe that anybody
Feels the way I do about you now.

Middle 2

All the roads that lead you there are winding
All the lights that light the way are blinding.
There are many things that I would
Like to say to you – but I don't know how —

Final chorus *(repeat ad lib.)*

I said maybe, you're gonna be the one who
saves me?
And after all – you're my Wonderwall.

Song format

INTRO
VERSE 1
VERSE 2
MIDDLE 1
CHORUS
VERSE 3
MIDDLE 2
FINAL CHORUS

Chord format

Verse and Intro

4/4	Am C	G D	INTRO (× 2) VERSE (× 4)

Middle

4/4	1 F G	2 Am Am	3 F G	4 Am Am
	5 F G	6 C Am	7 D D	8 D D

Chorus *Fine*

4/4	F Am	C Am	(× 4)

Busking patterns

A

B

Percussion

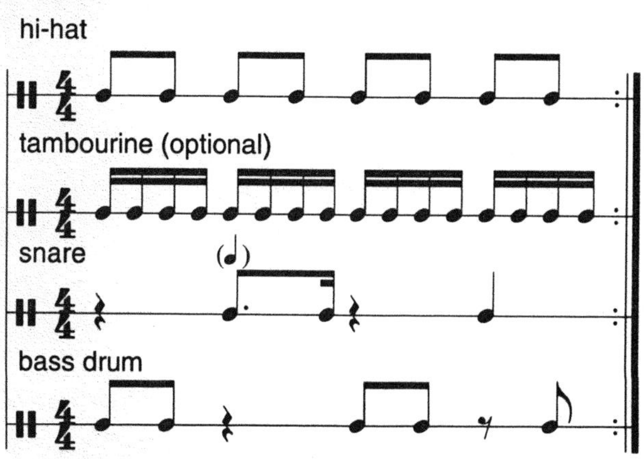

3 Project Good news medley

Source

This project uses three American folksongs, slightly modified, which share the same chord sequence and which can be sung simultaneously.

A *Good news* A spiritual, first notated in Fenner's *Religious folk songs of the Negro* in 1874.
B *Go tell Aunt Rhody* Also known as *Go tell Aunt Nancy*. Some claim the melody can be traced back to a 1752 opera by Rousseau.
C *He's got the whole world* First collected in the 1920s, this spiritual is popular world-wide.

Singing style

The songs should be rhythmic and fun and sung in an easy singing style, allowing for syncopation and portamento.

Teaching the songs

All three songs are easy to learn as they have repetitive words. Teach them separately by rote to the whole class and have the pupils learn the words as they sing.

Performing the songs

The exact format for each song and their combination is entirely up to you and the class. Each song can be sung through on its own or combined in any number.

Accompanying the songs

The piano part will work well on its own, but the addition of a bass instrument (doubling the piano left hand), off-beat chords and simple percussion will lift the pieces.

Follow-up work

1 Once the songs have been learned, a performance could involve staggered entry, careful dynamics and a classroom instrumental ensemble.

2 Pupils could invent new words for the songs, or could compose a melody of their own over this chord sequence.

3 Project
Good news medley

3 Project Good news medley

Pupil's sheet

Good news

1 Good news, chariot's a-comin', (x 3)
Don't leave me behind.

2 Good news, freedom is a-comin', (x 3) …

3 Good news, justice is a-comin', (x 3) …

4 Good news, equality is comin', (x 3) …

5 Good news, heaven is a-comin', (x 3) …

Go tell Aunt Rhody (Go tell Aunt Nancy)

1 Go tell Aunt Rhody, (x 3)
The old grey goose is dead.

2 The one she's been savin', (x 3)
To make her feather bed.

3 She died in the millpond, (x 3)
From standin' on her head.

He's got the whole world in his hands

1 He's got the whole world in his hands,
He's got the big wide world in his hands,
He's got the whole world in his hands,
He's got the whole world in his hands.

2 He's got you and me, brother, in his hands,
He's got you and me, sister, …
He's got you and me, brother, …

3 He's got the sun and the moon in his hands,
He's got the wind and the rain …
He's got the sun and the moon …

4 He's got the itty, bitty baby in his hands …

5 He's got everybody in his hands …

Own choice

6 He's got Manchester United/everyone in Scotland/the whole school in his hands …

Chord format

4/4

1 D	2 D	3 A7	4 D
5 D	6 D	7 A7	8 D

Coda

4/4

1 D

4 Project Only you

Source

Originally a hit from the 1960s, *Only you* by V. Clarke was made famous in the 1980s in an *a capella* arrangement by the Flying Pickets.

Singing style

The melody follows a stepwise downward path rather like a gentle scale exercise. It suits young people's voices very well and encourages clear, unforced singing. Make sure the long notes last and that the diction is clear.

Teaching the song

Teach this one from the piano with the pupils seated in a group nearby. Play the melody clearly, filling in some notes from the chords and with the bass line as written. Take time to show pupils how each verse fits the words once they have got the tune right on the first verse. The introduction is also the main tune of the descant, so everyone should learn it. The second part of the descant follows the melody in parallel thirds. However, the piece sounds well without the descant so don't get bogged down in it if you don't think it will work.

Follow-up work

1 Explain the term **descant** and what it means to harmonize in parallel thirds.

2 Listen to the Flying Pickets' recording and explain how the whole piece is performed **a capella**. This could introduce the class to the whole field of **unaccompanied singing**, from madrigals and sacred music to gospel, doo-wop and barbershop.

4 Project

Only you

V. Clarke arr. Patrick Allen

4 Project Only you

Pupil's sheet

4 Project Only you

V. Clarke arr. Patrick Allen

Introduction

Ba da da, ba da da, ba da da da, ba da da da
(x 2)

Verse

1 Looking from a window above,
It's like a story of love,
Can you hear me?
Came back only yesterday,
Moving further away,
Want you near me.

Chorus (after each verse)

All I needed was the love you gave,
All I needed for another day,
And all I ever knew – only you.

2 Sometimes when I think of your name
And it's only a game,
And I need you.
Listening to the words that you say,
Getting harder to stay,
When I see you.

3 This is gonna take a long time,
And I wonder what's mine,
Can't take no more.
Wonder if you'll understand,
It's just a touch of your hand,
Behind a closed door.

Chord format

Intro

4/4	1 C G/B	2 Am G	3 F	4 C G :‖

Verse

4/4	1 C G/B	2 Am G	3 F	4 C G
	5 C G/B	6 Am G	7 F	8 C G

Chorus

4/4	1 F	2 G	3 C	4 Am
	5 F	6 G	7 C	8 C

Note: When a chord is written thus: G/B the chord of G major is played with a B in the bass.

Percussion

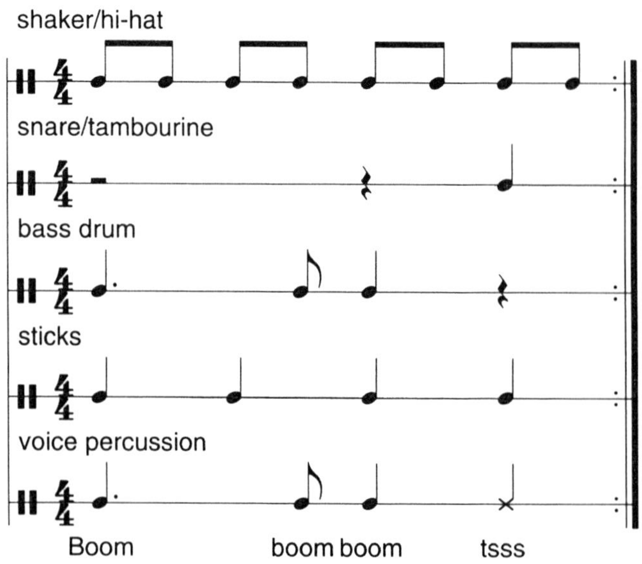

5 Project Two English folksongs

Source

Although there are so many published editions of English folksongs, they are usually written in keys inappropriate for this age group. These two have been chosen for their 'singability', range of notes and straightforward words.

A *The keeper* This is a Warwickshire folksong with an antiphonal chorus.
B *The miller of Dee* The melody of this song was probably composed in the seventeenth century, with words added a hundred years or so later.

Singing style

Both songs should be rhythmic and fun. These are country songs, not grand opera.

Teaching the songs

The keeper: This is great fun – give it a country dance feel with a light 'oom-pah' accompaniment. Begin by learning the chorus, since this involves sharing musical lines and phrases between two groups. Start it slowly and gradually speed it up so that the questions and answers really flow.
The miller of dee: Three of the four melodic lines are the same with only line three changing. The words have been altered slightly so that they fit the tune more easily. Keep the piece lively, even when learning it.

Performing the songs

Both songs would suit arranging for a small band, using piano/guitar, bass (synthesized or acoustic), keyboard and melody instruments and percussion. Make them sound fun, lively and danceable. Some may prefer *The keeper* in a higher key, so a transposition has been provided in C.

Follow-up work

1 *The miller of Dee* is a good song for introducing **6/8 rhythm** and the feel of **compound time signatures**. It shares its rhythm and origin with both *Lilliburlero* and *Greensleeves*, with which it could be compared. What other English folksongs do the pupils know? Their knowledge could be shared.

2 'Folk' material can be presented in a variety of ways to very different effects. It would be worth comparing authentic performances of folksongs by the Coppers, Martin Carthy or the Watersons, with orchestral settings, such as those by Vaughan Williams. The rock-folk settings of groups like Steeleye Span, Fairport Convention and Pentangle provide further variety and contrast.

3 The concept of a folk heritage should be introduced, where a song is transmitted through an oral rather than written tradition, altering as it passes through different times and communities. Have the pupils learned any songs this way?

4 *The keeper* has a melody based around arpeggios. Pupils may hear echoes of the hunting-call in this type of melody. The question and answer phrases in the chorus should be discussed. What was their effect? What was it like to sing them?

5 Project Two English folksongs

The keeper

English traditional

Busking pattern

5 Project Two English folksongs

The miller of Dee

English traditional

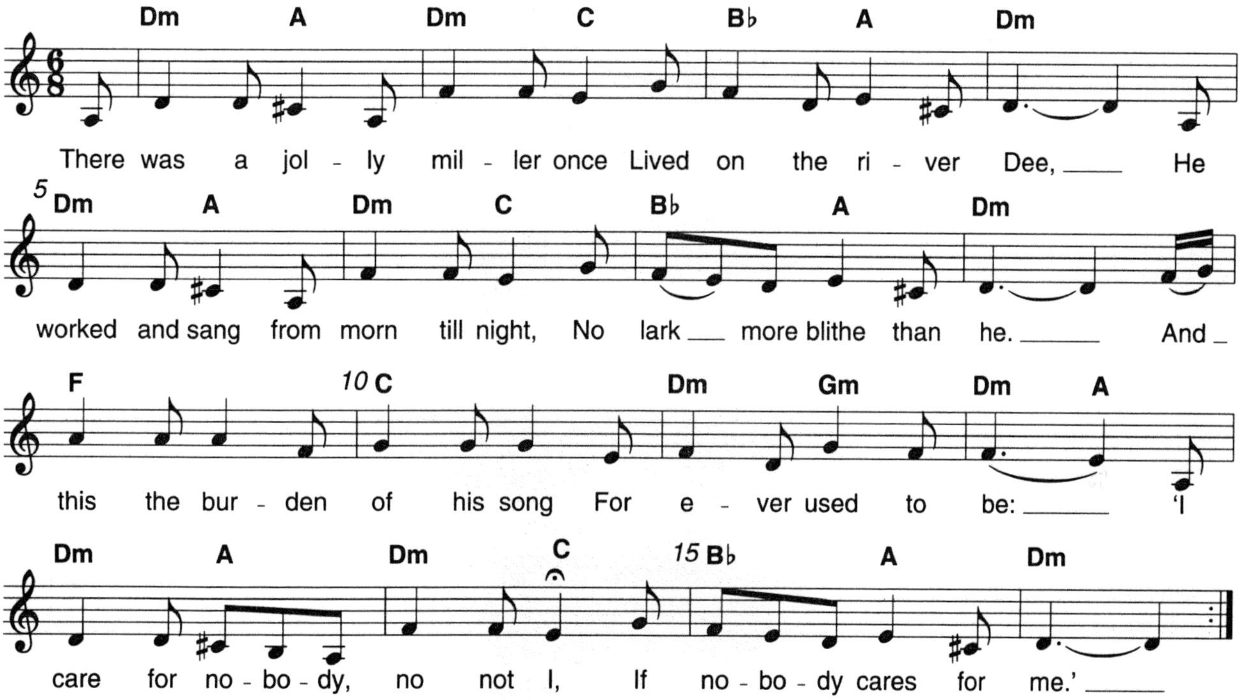

5 Project Two English folksongs

Pupil's sheet

The keeper

(English traditional)

1 The keeper did a-hunting go,
And under his cloak he carried a bow,
All for to shoot at the merry little doe,
Among the leaves so green-o.

Chorus (after each verse, in two groups)

A: Jackie boy!
B: Master!
A: Sing ye well?
B: Very well!
A: Hey down,
B: Ho down,
All: Derry, derry down,
Among the leaves so green-o.
A: To my hey down, down,
B: To my ho down, down,
A: Hey down,
B: Ho down,
All: Derry, derry down,
Among the leaves so green-o.

2 The first doe he shot at he missed,
The second doe he trimmed, he kissed;
The third doe went where nobody wist,
Among the leaves so green-o.

3 The fourth doe she did cross the plain,
The keeper fetched her back again,
Where she is now may she remain
Among the leaves so green-o.

Chord format

Verse

4/4

1 A	2 D A	3 A	4 D A	5 A	6 A E	7 F#m A	8 E A

Chorus

4/4

1 A	2 A	3 A	4 A E	5 F#m A	6 E A
7 A D A	8 A D A	9 A	10 A E	11 F#m A	12 E A

Transposition in C

Verse

4/4

1 C	2 F C	3 C	4 F C	5 C	6 C G	7 Am C	8 G C

Chorus

4/4

1 C	2 C	3 C	4 C G	5 Am C	6 G C
7 C F C	8 C F C	9 C	10 C G	11 Am C	12 G C

The miller of Dee

(English traditional)

1 There was a jolly miller once
Lived on the river Dee,
He worked and sang from morn till night,
No lark more blithe than he.
And this the burden of his song
For ever used to be:
'I care for nobody, no not I,
If nobody cares for me.'

2 'I love my mill, she is to me
Like parent, child and wife.
I would not change my dear old mill,
For any other life.
No lawyer, surgeon, doctor wise,
E'er had a groat from me.
I care for nobody, no not I,
If nobody cares for me.'

3 Then like the miller, bold and free,
Let us rejoice and sing.
The days of youth were made for glee,
And time is on the wing.
The song shall pass from me to thee,
And round this jovial ring.
We'll count our blessings one by one,
Then happily we shall sing.

Chord format

6/8

1 Dm A	2 Dm C	3 B♭ A	4 Dm
5 Dm A	6 Dm C	7 B♭ A	8 Dm
9 F	10 C	11 Dm Gm	12 Dm A
13 Dm A	14 Dm C	15 B♭ A	16 Dm

6 Project Rock and roll partners

This project tackles two rock and roll songs which share the same backing and can also harmonize with each other.

Rock around the clock

(Max C. Freedman/Jimmy De Knight)

Source

This song, performed by Bill Haley's Comets, launched rock and roll in 1955 when it was used as the background to the opening sequence of the film *The Blackboard Jungle*. It became the anthem of the younger generation and sold 22 million copies.

Singing style

This should be sung with exuberance and fun.

Teaching the song

The song can be learned easily. The problem generally comes in having a backing which is sufficiently simple and energetic to support the singing. In practice it is usually better just to play block chords, one per crotchet at the correct speed, rather than to attempt a complex backing slowly. The given bass line is optional. The hi-hat part is probably too difficult for most pupils at the correct speed, so one beat per crotchet will do, as long as we get those important 2nd and 4th beats on the snare! If you want the full backing with bass line, drums etc, then sequence it into your computer, or give pupils plenty of advance warning.

Performing the song

Go for energetic simplicity. The detail in the instrumental parts is optional, just so long as the chords and the main beat are there! There is scope for instrumental or vocal rhythmic improvisation (on C) if you leave one verse free for this.

At the hop

(Singer/Medora/White)

Source

This was released by Danny and the Juniors in 1957, and it describes the various dance crazes of the time.

Singing style

This should also be fun, but the verse has more words to fit in, so practise them slowly first.

Teaching the song

The chorus is very easy to learn and fits over the verse of *Rock around the clock*. The verse will take longer to learn, but could make a good solo or small group opportunity. There are also opportunities for backing vocals. The verse has the 'Hop hop hop hop' backing, and the chorus has a number of 'Oh, baby's. These are clearly outlined in the score and should be practised with the whole group first. Once again, life is made easier if you sequence the backing first.

Performing the song

At the hop is great fun to perform, with its simple backing vocals, straightforward chorus and opportunities for solos and small groups. Keep the backing fast and simple, emphasizing the off-beats (2 and 4).

Combining the songs

The two songs do fit on top of each other (except for the introduction), but it would be best to begin by just adding the chorus of *At the hop* to *Rock around the clock* until both songs are known really well by the class.

Follow-up work

1 Pupils could be taught the origins and outcomes of rock and roll, including its huge social impact. These songs still sound fresh and exciting and pupils could hear and discuss the original recordings.

2 Both songs are based on the 12-bar blues. Pupils should recognize the chord changes and become familiar with the wide range of musical styles which use this structure.

3 The 12-bar blues can form the basis for composition and improvisation work. If the backing is sequenced into the computer, pupils can invent melodies and songs over it.

6 Project Rock and roll partners

Rock around the clock

Max C. Freedman/Jimmy D. Knight

Rock and roll partners

At the hop

Singer/Medora/White

6 Project Rock and roll partners

Pupil's sheet

Rock around the clock

(Max C. Freedman/Jimmy Knight)

Introduction

One, two, three o'clock, four o'clock, rock.
Five, six, seven o'clock, eight o'clock, rock.
Nine, ten, eleven o'clock, twelve o'clock, rock,
We're gonna rock around the clock tonight.

Verse

1 Well put your glad rags on, join me, hun,
We'll have some fun when the clock strikes one.

Chorus (after each verse)

We're gonna rock around the clock tonight,
We're gonna rock, rock, rock till the broad daylight,
We're gonna rock, gonna rock around the clock tonight.

2 When the clock strikes two, three and four
If the band slows down we'll yell for more.

3 When the chimes ring five, six and seven
We'll be rockin' up in seventh heaven.

4 When it's eight nine, ten, eleven too
I'll be going strong with you.

5 When the clock strikes twelve, we'll cool off then
Start rockin' round the clock again.

Chord format

Rock around the clock

Intro

4/4

1 C	2 C	3 C	4 C
5 C	6 C	7 G G	8 G G

Rock around the clock/At the hop

Verse and Chorus

4/4

1 C	2 C	3 C	4 C
5 F	6 F	7 C	8 C
9 G	10 F	11 C	12 G

Coda

4/4

1 C

At the hop

(Singer/Medora/White)

Verse

1 Well you can rock it, you can roll it,
Do the stomp and even stroll it, at the hop.
When the record starts a-spinning,
You calypso when you chicken, at the hop.
Do the dance sensation that is sweeping the nation,
At the hop.

Chorus

Let's go to the hop! (Oh, baby) (x 4)
Oooh, aah, let's go to the hop!

2 Well you can swing it, you can groove it,
You can really start to move it, at the hop.
Well the jockey is the smoothest,
And the DJ is the coolest, at the hop.
All the cats and chicks can get their kicks,
At the hop.

6 Project Rock and roll partners

Pupil's sheet

Busking patterns

A

B
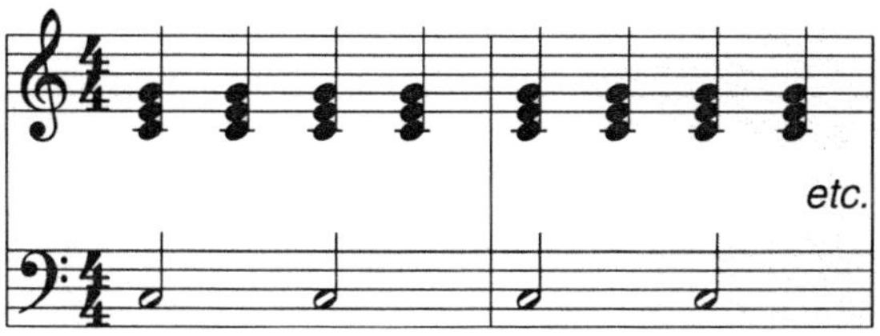

C

D

E

Note: The busking patterns need adapting to chord changes.

Rock around the clock

Song format

INTRO
VERSE
CHORUS (after each verse)

At the hop

Song format

VERSE 1
CHORUS
VERSE 2
CHORUS
VERSE 1
CHORUS × 2

Percussion

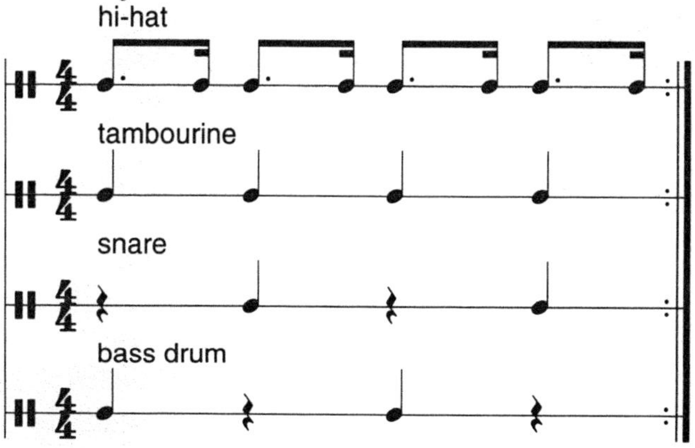

7 Project Two circle chants

Source

This project includes two native American chants now used in circle-dancing, a simple form of communal dance developed from a wide range of cultures and traditions and now practised world-wide.

Singing style

The pieces are strongly rhythmic and this should be felt by the whole body, in movement and clapping. Vary the dynamics as the class sing.

Teaching the songs

Both chants should be taught aurally and are best sung accompanied by just percussion or clapping. Simple chords can be added as suggested to help pitch and give confidence. The songs are simple, hypnotic in their effect and harmonize easily. They are best learned in a circle, perhaps as a prelude to another activity, and can be accompanied by simple movements as described below.

We circle around: This song will work in unison or with the harmony parts which can be sung in any octave, depending on the vocal ranges of class members. The second harmony part can, in particular, be sung an octave lower. The first harmony part is a direct parallel of the melody and is the easier of the two to work with.
Heya nana: This is a short chant using parallel harmonies in the mixolydian mode. It works both in unison and with either or both harmonies which can be sung in any octave. Two versions are provided to suit the vocal ranges of different classes. The chant can be sung repeating the first two bars, then repeating the last two bars. On the first time of the repeat, however, the last quaver of bar 2 should be omitted.

Performing the songs

Experiment with unison, harmony, staggered entry, varied percussion and clapping, as well as a wide variety of dynamics. Simple walking movements can be added if the group are in a circle. Pupils can try the following: in time to the music and in groups of four, with slow steps walk towards the centre of the circle and back; sidestep to left and right; march clockwise and anti-clockwise round the circle; turn slowly on the spot.

Other slow movements can be performed, led by any member of the circle, for example: crossing and uncrossing arms one by one across the chest; holding up palms one by one in front of body and lowering them again; raising arms above head and lowering them a beat at a time.

Follow-up work

1 The relationship between music and dance can be explored, from ritualistic music such as this to more sophisticated forms such as ballet. The modern dance trends such as techno, trance, dub and house have returned music to a tribal, ritualistic phase. How does dance enter the pupils' lives? What sorts of music make them want to dance?

2 Stravinsky's *Rite of spring* is a fascinating collision of sophistication, primitive ritual and ballet form. Pupils could be made aware of the complex orchestration and the primitive power of the piece. Play them the *Danse des adolescentes* and discuss their responses.

7 Project

Two circle chants

We circle around

Native American arr. Patrick Allen

Chord format

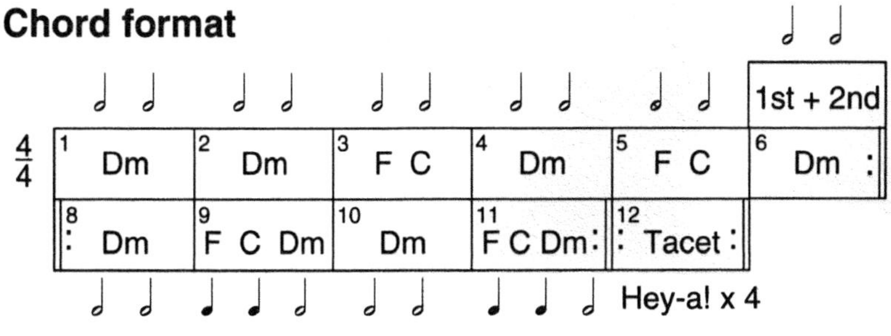

Percussion

7 Project Two circle chants

Heya nana

Native American arr. Patrick Allen

Chord format

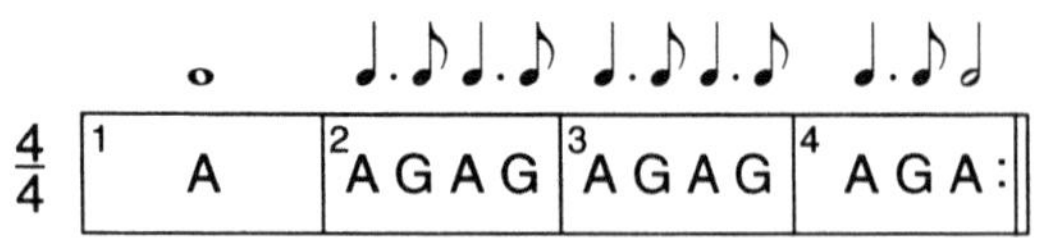

Percussion

Note: With some classes it works best by transposing the piece into D.

8 Project Swing low medley

Source

The songs in this project are linked in the manner of 'partner songs' and can be sung simultaneously. There are six component parts to this 'medley':

A *When the saints go marching in* A traditional North American spiritual with additional verses added by the author.
B *I wanna sing* A North American folksong.
C *Rolling along* A tune composed by the author in the manner of an American folksong, to a traditional lyric, completing the harmony.
D *Swing low, sweet chariot (verse)* A North American spiritual. The chorus is well known to English football fans.
E *Swing low, sweet chariot (chorus).*
F Piano/chord backing.

Singing style

All the songs should be sung rhythmically, with a sense of fun and in a free American folk style with scope for grace notes and portamentos. Allow for additional syncopation if the singers want to add it.

Using the medley

The songs can be sung individually or in any combination over the backing part which fits them all. It is particularly exciting when all the songs are running at once as this creates an easy-to-learn polyphony. The backing can easily be sequenced into your computer or, alternatively, it can be played by class members from the chord format. The medley should work well in an assembly or with combined classes, assigning groups to particular songs.

Teaching the songs

Both the verse and the chorus of *Swing low* fit the chord sequence, but when singing *Swing low* against the other songs it is easier to stick just to the chorus.

Strictly speaking the chord sequence is not exactly right for *When the saints go marching in* but bar 2 (which should be a D throughout) creates a delightful suspension which really adds character to the piece. Begin by teaching the songs in unison.

Next try dividing the group in half, starting with one song and then adding the second when the first is secure. Then subdivide as much as you can.

Performing the songs

The exact format for each song and their combination is entirely up to you and the class. A song can be sung through on its own or the songs can be combined in any number. An effective performance can be made from just three choruses. In this case group A begins with *Swing low*, group B with *When the saints go marching in* and group C with *I wanna sing*. After singing through their own chorus each group then moves to the next on the list so all the choruses are sung by each group, but at different times.

Accompanying the songs

Although the individual songs can be learned unaccompanied, you will really need the accompaniment to hold the polyphony together. Keep a firm beat. Percussion could be added or you could try doubling the piano bass line on another instrument.

Follow-up work

1 Tape-record a performance and get the class to evaluate their part-singing. Which parts were sung well? Were the tunes well-balanced? Could some be louder, softer, clearer, better pitched? Does it sound different hearing the piece, as opposed to performing it? How could the performance be improved?

2 Why do these songs work well against each other? What is **polyphony**? Play the class examples of polyphony from the Renaissance and later ages to demonstrate how the many different strands of music work with each other. The combined texts and melodies could also be compared with medieval motets where texts in different languages were sometimes combined.

3 Pupils could write new words for *When the saints go marching in* which are more relevant to their own worlds or aspirations.

8 Project

Swing low medley

arr. Patrick Allen

8 Project Swing low medley

8 Project Swing low medley

Pupil's sheet

When the saints go marching in

(North American spiritual)

1 Oh when the saints go marching in,
Oh when the saints go marching in,
I wanna be in that number,
When the saints go marching in.

2 (And) when the sun refuse to shine...

3 (And) when the world will live as one...

4 (And) on that hallelujah day...

5 (Oh) when the rivers can run pure...

6 (Oh) when the world is free from war...

I wanna sing

(North American folksong)

I wanna sing, sing, sing,
I wanna dance, dance, dance,
I wanna sing, I wanna dance, hallelu...
When the gates are open wide,
I'll be standing at your side,
I wanna sing, I wanna dance, hallelu...

Rolling along

Rolling along, singing this song,
Devil is after me,
Chariots of fire, songs reaching higher,
I know he won't catch me.

Swing low, sweet chariot

(North American spiritual)

Chorus (after each verse)

Swing low, sweet chariot,
Comin' for to carry me home. (Repeat)

Verse

1 I looked over Jordan and what did I see?
Comin' for to carry me home,
A band of angels comin' after me,
Comin' for to carry me home.

2 I'm sometimes up, and sometimes down,
Comin' for to carry me home,
But still I know I'm freedom bound,
Comin' for to carry me home.

3 If you get there before I do,
Comin' for to carry me home,
Tell all my friends that I'm coming too,
Comin' for to carry me home.

4 If I get there before you do,
Comin' for to carry me home,
I'll cut a hole and pull you through,
Comin' for to carry me home.

Chord format

4/4

1 D	2 G D	3 D	4 A (A7)
5 D D7	6 G D	7 D A	8 D

Coda

4/4

1 D

9 Project Two songs by Schubert

Two songs by Franz Schubert (1797–1828) transposed to keys suitable for whole class singing at KS3.

The trout (Die forelle)

Source

This song for voice and piano was composed in 1817 by Franz Schubert (1797–1828) (D550). He produced four versions, the last in 1821.

Singing style

The piece must be bright, clear and melodic, with the words clearly enunciated. The third verse needs a change in mood; but it is merely sad, not tragic as the river goes flowing on.

Teaching the song

Teach *The trout* in 4-bar sections, but keep it bright and rhythmic at all times. An optional modern rhythmic accompaniment is provided which keeps the light bounciness of the original, without altering the melody in any way. Pupils find this rhythm appealing, but it is best to use a more straightforward accompaniment while they are learning the tune. Simpler alternatives are provided.

Follow-up work

1 Once pupils know this melody they can approach a wide range of important listening and historical background work. By listening to a recording of the song they can compare their performance with that of a professional. They should focus attention on **singing style, quality of voice, interpretation** and the nature and purpose of the **accompaniment**. They will notice that verse three has a melody they do not recognize, to paint the capture of the trout. They will notice too that the **tempo** and manner of performance change at this point. In general they should also discuss the way the work reflects the character of the fish, the river and the tale in its melody, accompaniment and interpretation.

2 The **lied** as a song *genre* should be mentioned, particularly how the melody and its accompaniment respond to the verse set.

3 A recording of *The trout* piano quintet provides further useful listening work. The piece offers a set of **variations** on this theme and pupils can be expected to talk and write about each variation. They should focus on the **treatment of the melody**, the **instrumentation**, the **mood** or **character of each variation**, any **unexpected chords** or **modality**. Their initial response can be in grid form, followed by discussion and a prose response.

Cradle song (Wiegenlied)

Source

This lullaby (Op. 96) was composed by Schubert in 1816.

Singing style

Pure and melodic for the melody, warm and mellow for the harmony part. Sing it tenderly with plenty of *rubato*.

Teaching the song

Although not all the class may be able to sing this melody well, it is simple and can be quickly learned. If no one seems up to the melody, then get them to sing the harmony while you play the tune. The harmony part is on a single note, pitched so that all the class can manage it at an appropriate octave. Give the class the imaginary task of sending a child to sleep.

Follow-up work

1 This lullaby could be compared with *Allundé* (see Project 18) in terms of its purpose, effect and character. It is worth noting that *Allundé* works on the basis of a drone, while this song uses a dominant/tonic relationship throughout. Both songs are equally effective but through different means.

2 Using either a drone or dominant/tonic chords, pupils could compose pieces for a specific purpose or effect. This could be a lullaby, or groups could have tasks directing them to different ideas: work, warfare, healing, dancing, mourning, celebrating etc. A real challenge is provided when the same chord sequence or drone must be suitable for all different purposes.

9 Project Two songs by Schubert

The trout (Die forelle)

F. Schubert arr. Patrick Allen/Words: W. G. Rothery

Two songs by Schubert

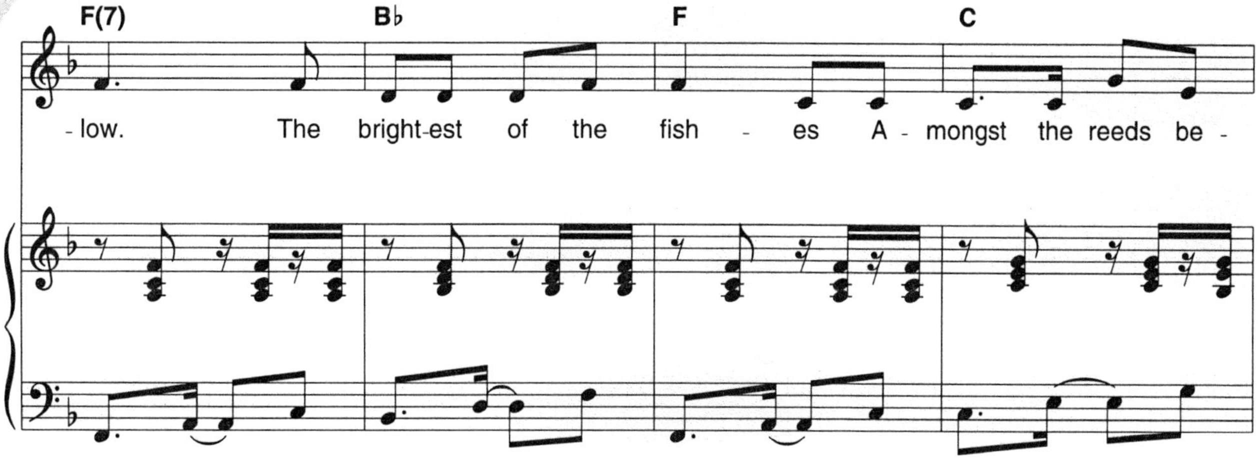

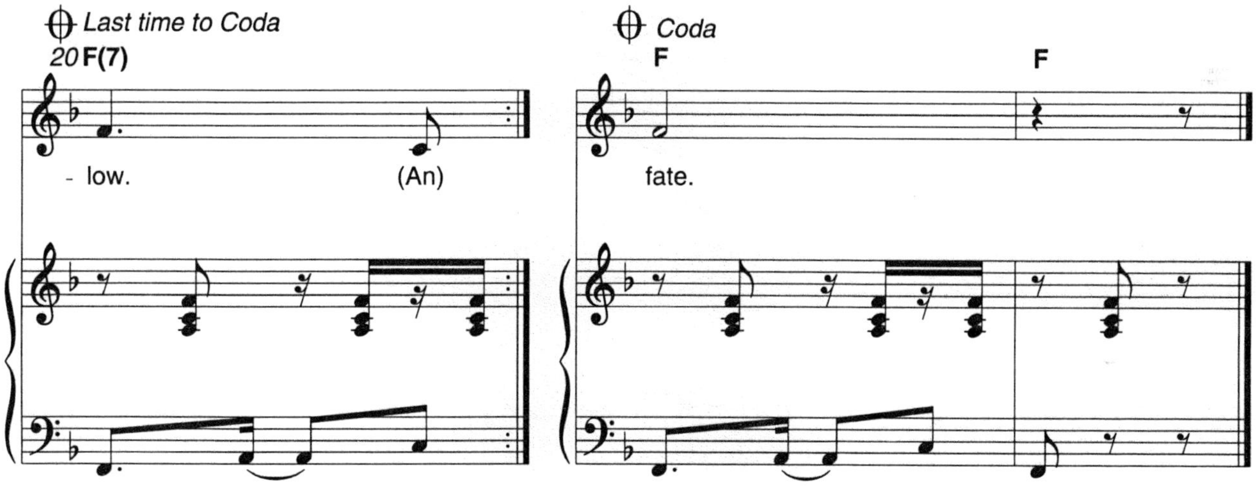

Busking patterns

9 Project Two songs by Schubert

Cradle song (Wiegenlied)

F. Schubert/Words: Patrick Allen

9 *Project*

Two songs by Schubert

Pupil's sheet

The trout

F. Schubert/Words: W. G. Rothery

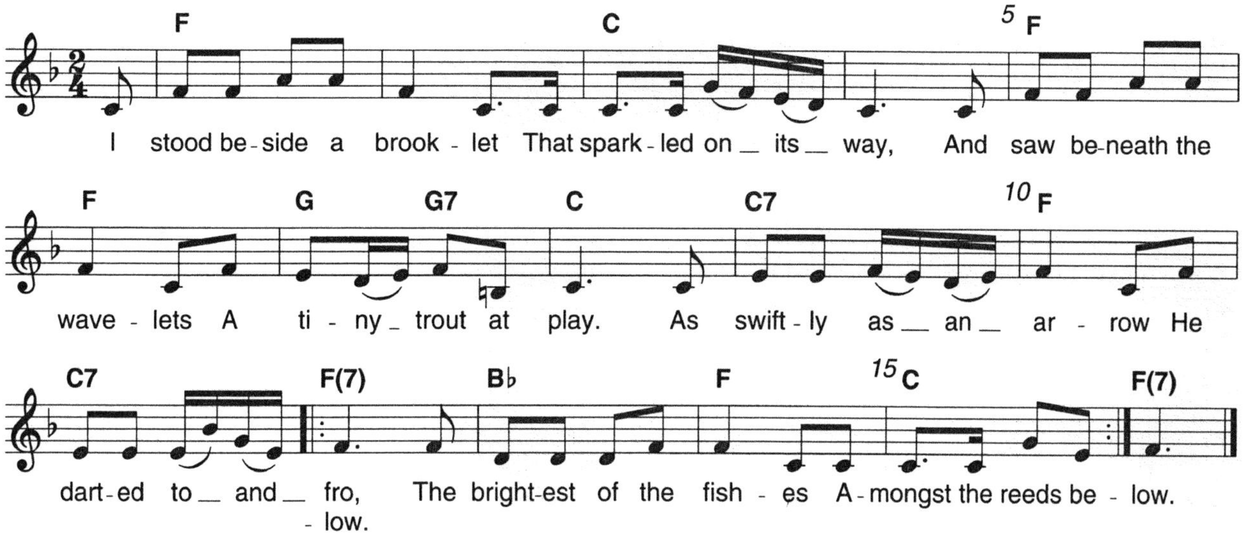

1 I stood beside a brooklet
That sparkled on its way,
And saw beneath the wavelets
A tiny trout at play.
As swiftly as an arrow
He darted to and fro,
The brightest of the fishes
Amongst the reeds below. } repeat

2 An angler there was standing
With rod and line in hand,
Intent upon the fishes
A sportive, fearless band.
'Tis vain,' said I, 'good neighbour,
To fish a brooklet clear,
The fish will surely see you
Upon the bank so near.' } repeat

3 But skilful was the angler
And he was artful too,
The crystal brook defiling
He hid the fish from view.
And then his skill renewing,
The fishes took the bait
And I was left lamenting
My tiny troutlet's fate. } repeat

Chord format

2/4

1 F	2 F	3 C	4 C
5 F	6 F	7 G G7	8 C
9 C7	10 F	11 C7	12 :F(7)
13 B♭	14 F	15 C :	16 F(7)

Coda

2/4

1 F	2 F

9 Project Two songs by Schubert

Pupil's sheet

Cradle song

F. Schubert/Words: Patrick Allen

Verse

1 Dream and slumber, night-time shades are calling;
Daytime passing, stars begin to shine.
Rest your weary head, join the land of dreams, and
Sleep now, sleep now, night-time calls you on.

Harmony

Night has come; go to sleep.

2 World at peace now, strife and trouble ending;
Daytime's problems further than the stars.
Time for dreaming, planning a brand new day, when
Night-time's peace will guide us all day long.

Harmony

Peace has come; world at rest.

Chord format

4/4

1 D A7	2 D A7	3 D A7	4 D A7 D
5 A D	6 D A7	7 D A7	8 D A7 D

10 Project Wimmoweh

Source

Known as *Mbube* and *The lion sleeps tonight*, this song, written by Solomon Linda and translated by Paul Campbell, springs from a Zulu singing tradition. *Mbube* was originally recorded in South Africa by Solomon Linda and the Evening Birds and was popularized by Pete Seeger. The word *mbube* (corrupted to *wimmoweh*) means 'lion': 'The lion king is sleeping'.

Singing style

The underlying triplet rhythm in this song is really important, although difficult to notate, and it is important that it feels relaxed and natural. ♩♪ (3) is notated as ♪.♬ throughout. As with many of the songs in this pack this is easier to sing than to read. The harmony parts should be balanced and the melodies should soar through them.

Teaching the song

The piano part can just keep running with simple instrumental and percussion parts added *ad lib*. This could be done using the computer so that you are free to teach the parts. Choose your verse singers before the lesson starts. A step-by-step approach is suggested:

i get everybody to sing the 'bass line' at their own pitch in order to feel the foundation of the harmony. Then get everyone to sing the other two harmonies. At this stage sing to 'oooh, aaah'

ii now start dividing the harmonies. Try to keep everyone singing all the time

iii once the harmonies are running, introduce the vocalizations and rhythmic phrases to the harmony parts to liven them up. These can be allocated to any parts. In vocalization 4, the class can be divided into two halves – A and B, with B echoing A's vocalization

iv practise parts coming in and out, building and thinning the texture and changing the chants and vocalizing sounds. This is immensely satisfying, so keep it going as long as you like

v to introduce the tune, play it or sing it yourself so the whole class is backing you

vi get your melody singers to join in.

Follow-up work

Create a structured performance using staggered entries of harmony parts, the melodies and a small classroom instrumental ensemble. Get the pupils to devise the overall structure. Pupils can invent:

i their own rhythmic vocalizations to the existing harmony notes

ii their own harmonies and melodies over the chord sequence, first using semibreves, then minims and crotchets, and finally free improvisation.

Once the pupils feel the harmony well they can invent freely, leading on to melody writing over the backing, using 4- or 8-bar phrases.

10 Project

Wimmoweh

Linda/Campbell arr. Patrick Allen

Vocalizations and rhythms for harmony parts

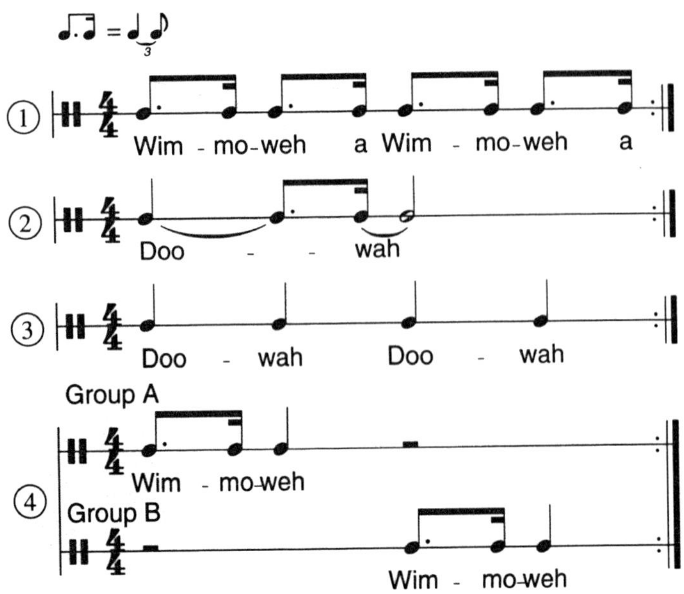

10 Project Wimmoweh

Pupil's sheet

Linda/Campbell arr. Patrick Allen
Words: Peretti, Creatori, Weiss, Stanton

1 In the jungle, the mighty jungle, the lion sleeps tonight,
In the jungle, the quiet jungle, the lion sleeps tonight.

2 Near the village, the peaceful village, the lion sleeps tonight, …

3 Hush, my darling, don't fear, my darling, the lion sleeps tonight, …

Chord format

4/4

1	2	3	4
G	Am/C	G/D	D7

Note: When a chord is written thus: Am/C the chord of A minor is played with a C in the bass; and when it is written thus: G/D the chord of G major is played with a D in the bass.

Percussion

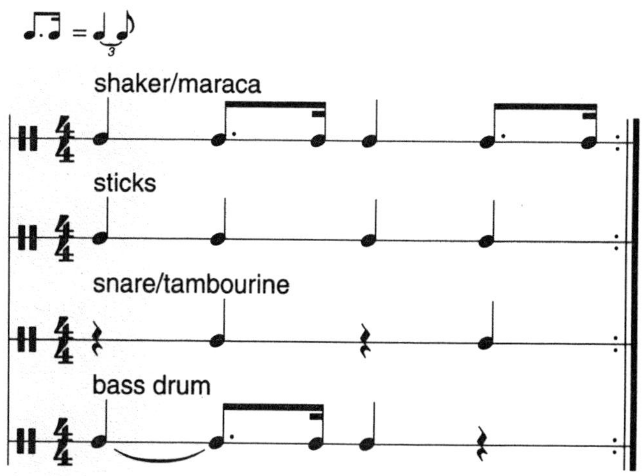

11 Project Love is all around

Source

In 1967, the 'Summer of Love', The Troggs reached No.5 in the UK and No.7 in the US pop charts with this song, *Love is all around* by R. Presley, a big contrast to their earlier hit, *Wild thing*. The song had even greater success more than twenty-five years later when Wet, Wet, Wet released a cover version as part of the soundtrack for the film *Four Weddings and a Funeral*.

Singing style

The song is gentle and melodic. The chorus can be both louder and stronger than the verse.

Teaching the song

Most pupils seem to know this song already and it can be taught very quickly. If you teach it with the accompaniment, you will find the gaps in the verse are useful for instructions and for announcing the next line of lyrics. There are often details of the melody and syncopations which will need clarifying.

As with the other songs in this pack, *Love is all around* will work on its own or with any of the harmony parts. The harmony part printed above the main tune works in rhythmic parallel with the melody on a very limited number of notes. A chosen group can learn it quickly once the main melody is known. The part is very repetitive, simple and effective and can be sung in any octave.

Two ostinato parts (riffs) which can be sung (or played) throughout the verse are provided. These fill in the long gaps in the melody very well. There are three simple four-note patterns (the 'ooh' parts) which can be repeated over the verse singly or in combination.

Accompanying the song

The first busking pattern sets the style for any accompaniment on piano, guitar, or by the class. The song is ideally suited to class ensemble performance involving singing and playing. A full arrangement would include chords, bass, drums, melody and any of the vocal harmonies, perhaps doubled on instruments.

Follow-up work

1 Record and evaluate your whole class performance of this song.

2 Using the chords of *Love is all around*, create your own chord sequence as the basis for a song.

11 Project

Love is all around

R. Presley arr. Patrick Allen

11 Project Love is all around

Busking patterns

A

B

Note: The busking patterns will need to adapt to chord changes in the verse. The same rhythmic pattern will apply.

11 Project Love is all around

Pupil's sheet

R. Presley arr. Patrick Allen

Verse

1 I feel it in my fingers, I feel it in my toes.
Love is all around me and so the feeling grows.

2 It's written on the wind, it's everywhere I go.
If you really love me, come on and let it show.

Chorus

You know I love you, I always will,
My mind's made up by the way that I feel.
There's no beginning, there'll be no end,
'Cos on my love you can depend.

3 I see your face before me, as I lay on my bed.
I kind of got to thinking of all the things you said.

4 You gave your promise to me, and I gave mine to you.
I need someone beside me in everything I do.

Song format

VERSE 1
VERSE 2
CHORUS
VERSE 3
VERSE 4
CHORUS
VERSE 1
VERSE 2
CODA

Vocal riffs for verse

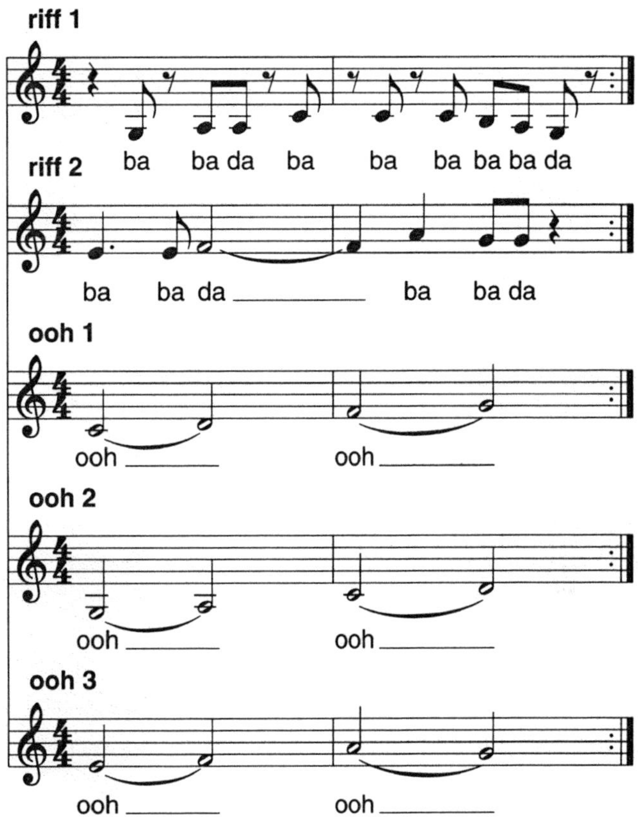

Percussion

Chord format

Verse (4/4)

1	2	3	4
C Dm	F G	C Dm	F G

Chorus (4/4)

1	2	3	4	5
F	Dm	F	C	F
6 Dm	7 Dm	8 G	9 G	

Coda (4/4)

1	2
F G	C

12 Project Three lions

Source

This was the official song of the England football team in Euro 96 and was written by Ian Broudie and recorded originally by Baddiel, Skinner and the Lightning Seeds on Epic Records. The song has been transposed to suit pupils at Key Stage 3.

Singing style

Football terrace style with a few refinements, notably giving notes their full value and sound pitch!

Teaching the song

The refrain of this song is known round the world and has entered into the folk repertoire of football fans in a number of versions. The verse is less well known and will need learning separately. How thoughtful of Ian Broudie to write a refrain which everyone knows *and* which harmonizes! The verse could be a good opportunity for solos or groups to sing.

Performing the song

This can be a piano/guitar sing-along or a whole class performance with students both playing and singing. The accompaniment has a chugging rhythm all the way through, although the texture thins in the middle sections. The instrumental bass line is particularly important in this song and needs to come across clearly. In the original a simplified version of refrain A is used at the beginning and after the middle. The format is possibly confusing, particularly the occurrences of refrains A and B. Refrain A occurs at the beginning and after the middle section, refrain B after each verse. The two combine at the end. It is possible to get effective dynamic contrasts in this piece, especially after the vocal middle where refrain A should begin very quietly, gradually increasing in volume until refrain B joins in. This section can develop from *pp* → *f*.

Follow-up work

1 Talk about why it is important for a team to have a musical focus for its members and supporters. What qualities should it have? What other sports/supporters' songs do pupils know?

2 Not only sports teams have tunes to build identity and morale. In what other context does music provide a focus of identity and feeling? Pupils may think of the armed services, regiments, nations, regions, schools and universities, religions. Discussion may follow on patriotic songs, military music, tribes and identity. There is a link, too, with the world of business and the media. Companies have adopted songs to identify themselves or their product in advertising and television and radio stations invent musical identities to represent themselves.

3 Pupils could evaluate the original recording. Although very singable, this is an untypical national football song, being rather nostalgic and tender and not at all tub-thumping or jingoistic. The recording itself is worth analysing in terms of a careful emotional build-up, changing texture and dynamics, use of sampled football crowds to create rhythm, instrumentation and untutored singing style. The use of counter-melodies with refrains A and B is worth identifying, as well as the descending bass line, a common trait in both Baroque music and English pop, especially The Beatles. Pupils could listen to the bass line in *Air on a G string* (2nd movement *Suite no. 3 in D*) by J. S. Bach, comparing this with *Penny Lane* by The Beatles.

12 Project Three lions

Broudie/Baddiel/Skinner arr. Patrick Allen

12 Project Three lions

12 Project Three lions

Pupil's sheet

Broudie/Baddiel/Skinner

Refrain A

(It's coming home), it's coming home,
It's coming, football's coming home. (x 2)

Refrain B

Three lions on a shirt, Jules Rimet still gleaming,
Thirty years of hurt, never stopped me dreaming.

Verse

1 Everyone seems to know the score,
They've seen it all before,
They just know, they're so sure
That England's going to throw it away,
Gonna blow it away,
But I know they can play,
'Cos I remember:

2 So many jokes, so many sneers,
But all those oh-so-nears
Wear you down
Through the years.
But I still see that tackle by Moore,
And when Lineker scored,
Bobby belting the ball
And Nobby dancing:

Vocal middle

I know that was then but it could be again …

Song format

INTRODUCTION
REFRAIN A (x 2)
VERSE 1
REFRAIN B
VERSE 2
REFRAIN B
INSTRUMENTAL MIDDLE
VOCAL MIDDLE
REFRAIN A
REFRAINS A and B
(repeat ad. lib)
CODA

Busking pattern

Chord format

Introduction and Refrains A and B

4/4	1	2	3	4
Chord	F C	Dm G	C C	Am C :
Bass Note	F E	D G	C B	A G :

→ Verse 1
→ Verse 2
→ Middle
→ Coda

Verse

4/4			
1 Dm	2 G	3 C	4 A
5 Dm	6 G	7 C	8 A
9 Dm	10 G	11 C	12 A

→ Refrain B

Instrumental middle

4/4			
1 Dm	2 B♭	3 Em	4 A :

Vocal middle

4/4			
1 Dm	2 B♭	3 A	4 A

→ Refrain A

Coda

4/4		
1 F C	2 Dm G	3 C

Simplified refrain A (optional)

4/4			
1 F	2 F	3 C	4 C

13 Project Asikatali

Source

Originally sung on South African picket lines, this song arrived in the US in the 1950s. It has been recorded by the Spinners and Pete Seeger.

Singing style

The 3/4 time needs to be felt clearly and pupils should be very accurate with the syncopations.

Teaching the song

There is no need to learn this all in one go. The melody and words can be taught first and the harmonies added later. Chant the words in small sections to the class, strictly in time with the rhythm of the song, gradually memorizing the words and the rhythm. As soon as they've grasped a line of words, teach pupils the melody and then progress to the next line. Add both lines together, so the whole class knows the melody. It helps to play the chords whilst learning the song. The words have been written out phonetically: 'u' is pronounced 'oo'.

The harmony line is a natural parallel to the melody in the first half and can be learned easily. The second half works on a basis of 'call and response' with the melody providing the 'call' and the other parts the 'response'. The bass line can be sung at the written pitch or an octave lower and uses just two notes. It follows the rhythm of the harmony line and is best learned alongside it. Use hand positions if necessary to indicate which of the two notes is being sung.

Performing the song

Although in performance the song sounds best unaccompanied, it can also work well with instruments playing the chords.

Follow-up work

1 This is a song of protest, arising from the struggle for human rights in South Africa. Pupils could be made aware of the role of music in the quest for justice, equality and freedom. The years of depression, war and social unrest in this century have produced a huge range of songs from utopian statements such as *The international* to folk songs like *We shall overcome* and *We shall not be moved*. Oppression during World War II produced songs such as *Bella ciao*, sung by Italian partisans. Woody Guthrie's songs championed the poor in the late 1930s and 1940s and influenced the American 'protest' singers of the 1960s, Pete Seeger, Joan Baez and Bob Dylan, who wrote at the time of the American Civil Rights Movement and the Vietnam War.

2 The song could be used as a good introduction to African music in general, highlighting the techniques of **parallel harmony in thirds** and **call and response**.

Asikatali

Pupil's sheet

South African arr. Patrick Allen

1 A-si-ka ta-li no-mas'ya baw-zwa si-zi-mi-se-li n-lu-le-ko (repeat)
Un-zi-ma lom-twa-lo u-fu-na-m(a) do-do (repeat)

2 We are the children of Africa, it's for freedom that we're fighting now, (repeat)

Melody: A heavy load, a heavy load – and it will take some strong souls (repeat)
Harmony: Heavy load a heavy load it will take some strong souls (repeat)

3 We shall not cease in our fight for justice, we shall march together hand in hand, (repeat)

Melody: A heavy load … (repeat)
Harmony: Heavy … (repeat)

Chord format

Verse

A-si-ka- ta-li *etc.*

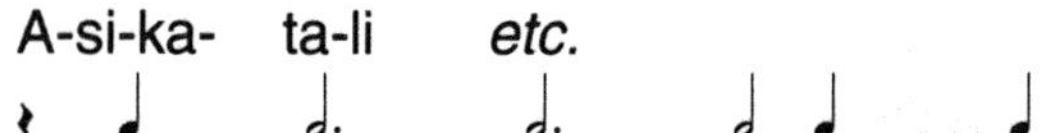

3/4

1	2	3	4	5
(C) G7	C	G7	C G7	C

Refrain

Un-zi- ma *etc.*

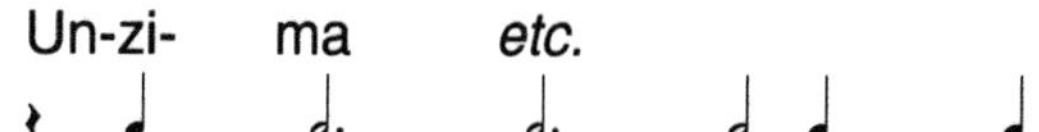

3/4

1	2	3	4	5
(C) G7	C	G7	C G7	C

14 Project Three sea songs

The songs in this project are 'shanties', sung at sea and on shore by British, Irish and American sailors. Most widely sung in the eighteenth and nineteenth centuries, they accompanied work and were derived from British folksongs and fiddle tunes, and some African chants.

Singing style

These are best learned and sung without guitar or piano accompaniment. Melody instruments could double the vocal parts. They should be sung vigorously with a strident vocal tone. Shanties would have been sung on deck in noisy and physically demanding circumstances so the delivery should avoid over-refinement, aiming to capture the rhythmic, work-based and convivial nature of the pieces. There is plenty of scope for portamento and grace notes for a performance in a true 'folk' style. The printed notes are, essentially, only an approximation.

Haul away, Joe

Source

A British foresheet shanty, sung while the sails were being hauled, consisting of a simple call and response.

Teaching the song

Teach the response first, getting the class to echo your singing. Sing the call in single line segments when you are teaching it, once again getting the class to echo you.

Performing the song

The 'call' can be sung by soloists or small groups and the response by everyone. The song works well with or without harmony, particularly if the class sway and clap (on and off-beat) to the rhythm. It is a work song and reflects the rhythm of working.

Leave her, Johnny

Source

Another British sea shanty, about the end of a tough voyage and the prospect of shore and pay.

Teaching the song

Teach a line at a time with the class echoing you.

Performing the song

This song will also sound more effective, and be more authentic, if the calls are taken by soloists or small groups. Once again the harmony is optional.

Turn the glasses over

Source

An American singing game with nautical origins.

Teaching the song

Teach the song a line at a time, repeating as many times as necessary and gradually increasing the length of the extracts the pupils sing from memory. Teach it at the correct speed (♩ = 155) from the outset.

Performing the song

This should be fast and rhythmic and sung like a dance tune. Pupils sometimes get confused with the number of 'over's so make them put up a thumb and fingers for each so they know they've done three. The vocal ostinato is easy and adds rhythmic punch. The counter-melody, which can be played or sung, is also quite simple, but the song works perfectly well without it. Everyone can clap the 'simple' part whilst singing, but the other clapping part is difficult and should be given to a separate group, if used.

Follow-up work

1 Pupils could investigate sea shanties further and links could be made with geography and history, to explore the work and conditions of seamen in the eighteenth and nineteenth centuries. Shanties unified the effort on board ship and often had words improvised on topical subjects by the 'shanty man' who led the singing. Pupils could consider why they are still good for binding groups and how we accompany our work with music today. The technique of call and response could be compared with their study of African and gospel music.
2 Pupils could invent modern or topical words for the shanties or develop their own work songs.
3 Famous recordings of shanties include those by Ewan MacColl, A. L. Lloyd and the Clancy Brothers. The *Fantasia on British sea songs* by Henry Wood is the crowning moment of the Last Night of the Proms and features nine British sea songs, attributed and traditional.

14 Project Three sea songs

Pupil's sheet

Haul away, Joe

1 Way, haul away, the good ship is a-bowlin'.
Way, haul away, haul away Joe.
(after each verse)
2 Way, haul away, we'll hang and haul together.
3 Way, haul away, we'll haul for better weather.
4 King Louis was the King of France before the revolution.
5 Louis got his head cut off and spoiled his constitution.
6 When I was a little lad, and so my mother told me.
7 That if I did not kiss the girls my lips would grow all mouldy.
8 The cook is in the galley, making pie so handy.
9 The captain's in his cabin, drinkin' wine and brandy.
10 Way, haul away, the good ship is a-bowlin'.

Leave her, Johnny

1 I thought I heard the captain say:
'Leave her, Johnny, leave her!
Tomorrow you will get your pay.
It's time for us to leave her.'

2 The work was hard and the passage long,
Leave her …
The seas were high and the gales were strong.
It's time …

3 The food was bad and the wages low,
Leave her …
But now ashore again we'll go.
It's time …

4 The sails are furled and our work is done,
Leave her …
And now on shore we'll have some fun.
It's time …

14 Project Three sea songs

Pupil's sheet

Turn the glasses over

Percussion

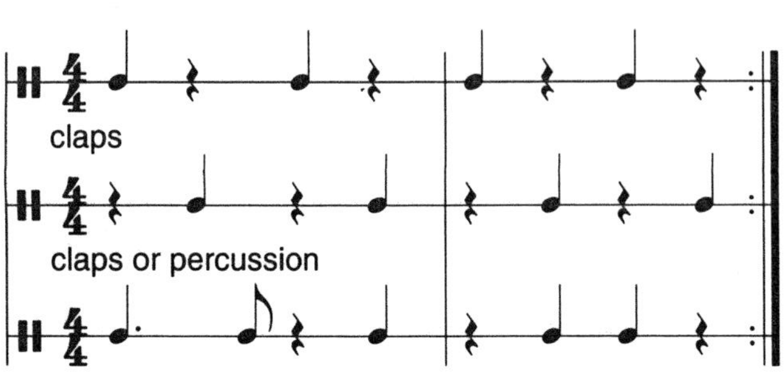

Vocal ostinato

15 Project Rivers of Babylon

Source

This biblical text (Psalm 137) is set by Brent Dowe and Trevor MacNaughton and was first recorded by the reggae group The Melodeons. Other well known versions are by Jimmy Cliff and Boney M.

Singing style

If the pupils alter the melody because they know the song from another version – let them! The piece needs a strong rhythmic accompaniment to work properly.

Teaching the song

The pupils probably know the tune, but still go through it with them to make sure they all sing the same version. Having the drum pattern running will help. The harmony begins on a single note and moves only slightly, following the melody when it does. If even this is too great a challenge the single note A works almost all the way through.

Accompanying the song

The busking pattern on the pupil sheet will form the basis of an effective accompaniment, using the off-beat reggae rhythms for the chords and the slow arpeggio pattern for the bass line. However, for the first bar of each section the rhythmic pattern stops and a held chord is used.

Follow-up work

The accompaniment is reggae based. Pupils will be able to provide examples of reggae songs and performers, but should also understand that reggae is a pop/rock form from the West Indies which developed from calypso combined with rhythm 'n' blues. In listening to reggae they should notice the free and flexible singing style, which was originally in Jamaican Creole, and the characteristic rhythmic underpinning of reggae.

A whole rastafarian culture is linked to reggae music through its leading exponent, Bob Marley. The class should be made aware of him and his influence. The connection between the lyrics of this song and the condition of slavery in the New World should also be clarified. The human and musical consequences of this enforced mass migration have been enormous and pupils should know that modern popular music is one of it outcomes.

15 Project

Rivers of Babylon

Dowe, MacNaughton arr. Patrick Allen

15 Project Rivers of Babylon

15 Project Rivers of Babylon

Pupil's sheet

Dowe, MacNaughton arr. Patrick Allen

Chorus

By the rivers of Babylon, there we sat down,
And there we wept when we remember'd Zion.
(repeat)

Verse

There the wicked carried us away captivity,
Require of us a song. Now how shall we sing you
The Lord's song in a strange land?

Middle

Let the words of our song
And the meditation of our hearts,
Be acceptable in Thy sight over I. (repeat)

Song format

CHORUS (x 2)
VERSE
CHORUS (x 2)
VERSE
CHORUS (x 2)
MIDDLE (x 2)
CHORUS (x 2)
CODA

Chord format

Chorus

etc.

4/4

1 D	2 D	3 D	4 D
5 D	6 A7	7 A7	8 D

Verse*

etc.

4/4

1 D	2 D	3 D	4 G	5 D
6 D	7 D	8 A7	9 D	

Middle*

etc.

4/4

1 D A	2 D	3 A	4 D
5 A	6 D	7 A	8 D

Coda*

4/4

1 D

**Note: Interrupt busking rhythm on first bar of each section and replace with held chords. Busking rhythm begins on second bar of each section.*

Busking pattern

Note: Throughout – except for first bar of each section where held chords are played. This rhythm is played from bar 2 onwards.

Percussion

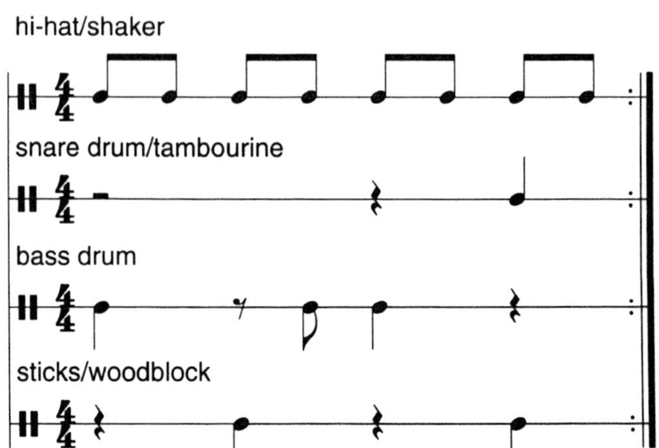

16 Project Two Native American chants

Huron war dance

This project includes two chants associated with rituals from the Native American tradition, which have been rearranged for classroom use.

Source

This is based on a Huron war dance from Canada.

Singing style

Strongly rhythmic, the lowest chant should have a solid, virile quality, with the final Hey! almost shouted. The middle chant is steadily rhythmic, with an accented first beat, while the top chant is like a cry, meaning 'On to war!'.

Teaching the song

Pupils should learn this aurally, starting with the drum and layering the parts from the lowest up. The whole chant should be continuously repeated until the parts are thoroughly learned. The piece may need transposing up for some classes.

Performing the song

The order of entry of the parts, the tempo, and the dynamics can all be altered during performance, depending on the class and their intentions with the piece. For example, it could represent a story: discovery of the enemy, sudden attack and then a cry of victory. A class member, or the teacher, could direct the changes.

Song of fire

Source

This is a simplified version of a piece developed from Navajo chants with Ifield Community College Choir. It is a ritual piece for a ceremony based around fire.

Singing style

This is equally rhythmic, but less aggressive than the Huron war dance. The main chant can be really strong.

Teaching the song

The main chant should be sung at the written pitch, but the other parts can be sung in any octave. Not all the parts are needed to make it work; quite a lot can be done with just the main chant and drums. The bass part in particular sounds well an octave higher. Start with the drum and the drone piano. If you have a synthesizer which can reinforce the drone with a low sustained note, even better. The parts should be learned aurally and in any order. Once a part is learned, leave it running and teach another part on top of it. Experiment bringing parts in and out and altering the dynamics by gesture.

Performing the song

Decide, with the class, on a structure and dynamic shape for the piece. Choose a class member to cue the entries and dynamic control, or make pupils memorize the order of events.

Follow-up work

Divide the class into groups of four or five. Each group is a 'tribe' with a special power and purpose: there are healers, magicians, warriors, carers, workers, hunters. Using chanting and percussion (pitched instruments can be used for a drone), each tribe must make up some ritual music for its special ceremony. The music must reflect the activities or aspirations of the group and the instruments should be chosen accordingly. Hold a grand ceremony at the end where each sub-tribe brings back its ritual music to the class. There should be some evaluation at the end, assessing particularly the appropriateness of the music to its purpose.

16 Project Two Native American chants

Huron war dance

Traditional arr. Patrick Allen

16 Project Two Native American chants

Song of fire

Traditional arr. Patrick Allen

17 Project Barbara Ann

Source

Composed in 1961 by Fred Fassert, this song was made famous by the Beach Boys in 1965.

Singing style

This song should be rhythmic and fun. It uses a very narrow range of notes but can be very effective with its simple harmonies and syncopated rhythm.

Teaching the song

This is a song with which many pupils are familiar. However, in the layered harmonies and improvisatory style of the Beach Boys' version, the distinction between the melody and harmony is sometimes unclear. Here, therefore, the song has been simplified to two very definite parts which may or may not coincide with pupils' recollection of the piece. It will therefore be necessary to re-teach the song to the class in small sections, keeping the two parts distinct from each other. If you can, teach the parts separately at first.

Part 1: This is essentially the melody line. It works both with and against the second part, generally a third higher. There is a danger the singers will be dragged down to the lower part when they work homophonically, especially on the 'Barb'ra Ann' riff, so in the early stages they will need reminding frequently of their note.
Part 2: This part provides both the main riff and a simple harmony to the melody. It only uses two notes so it should not provide too great a challenge. Pupils can either follow a copy of the vocal score or the lyric sheet which arranges the words of the two parts in relation to each other.

Performing the song

When learned, the song should really move (about ♩=145), with the accompaniment providing a simple chordal and rhythmic basis for the syncopated singing. The percussion needs to provide a fast and steady beat, accenting the off-beat.

Follow-up work

1 Listening to the Beach Boys' version, pupils will notice the *falsetto* singing. This is an accepted practice in certain pop-styles – soul, doo-wop and rock. The Bee Gees made particular use of this vocal range. It has parallels with the singing of counter-tenors and male altos in sacred and secular music up to the eighteenth century, in cathedral choirs, and in a twentieth-century revival spearheaded by Alfred Deller and James Bowman. Pupils could be introduced to the **male alto/counter-tenor** voice in sacred music and in solos from modern recordings of Handel and Purcell. Its historical purpose and origins could be explained. Some people find the voice disconcerting, whereas others note an almost instrumental purity in it.

2 The Beach Boys were famous for their vocal harmony, a close-harmony style using full-throated sound and some polyphonic techniques, adventurous in popular music of the time. Pupils could hear recordings of *Good vibrations* and *I get around* to hear their intricate harmonies at work. The concepts of **parallel harmony, independent parts, counter-melody**, and **polyphony** could be introduced to the class from both their listening and their experience of performing *Barbara Ann*.

17 Project

Barbara Ann

Pupil's sheet

Fred Fassert arr. Patrick Allen

17 Project Barbara Ann

Pupil's sheet

Busking patterns

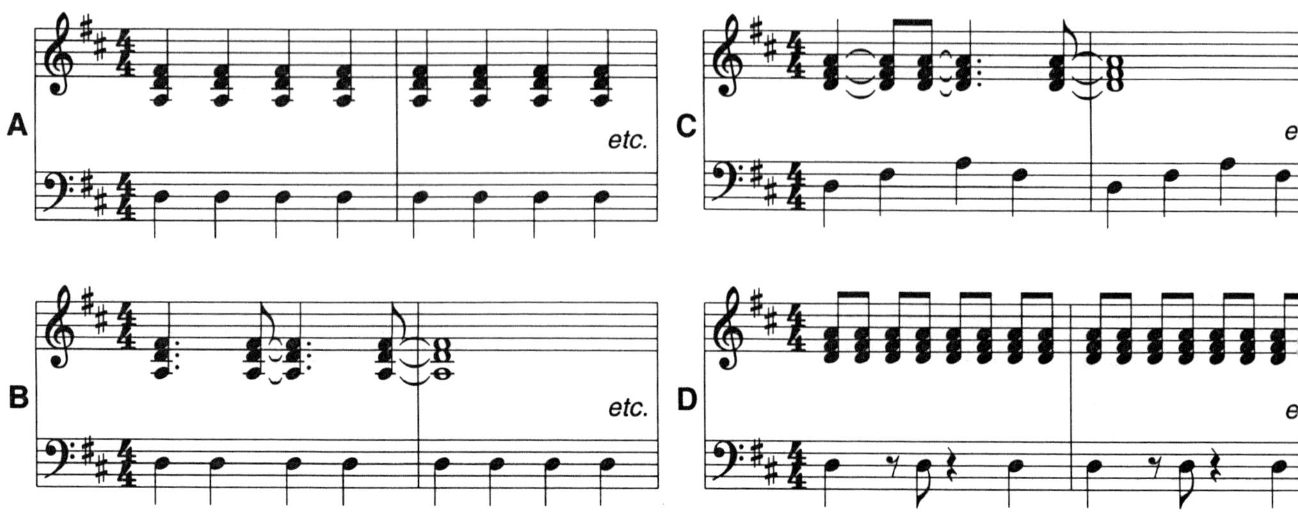

17 Project Barbara Ann

Pupil's sheet

Fred Fassert

Introduction/Chorus (both parts sung together)

1 Barb'ra
2 Bar, bar, bar, bar, Barb'ra Ann, Bar, bar, bar, bar, Barb'ra Ann,

1 Ann, Take my hand, Barb'ra
2 Bar, bar, bar, bar, Barb'ra Ann, Bar, bar, bar, bar, Barb'ra Ann,

1 Ann, You got me rockin' and a rollin',
2 Bar, bar, bar, bar, Barb'ra Ann. You got me rockin' and a rollin',

1 Rockin' and a rollin', Barb'ra Ann, Bar, bar, bar, Barb'ra Ann.
2 Rockin' and a rollin', Barb'ra Ann, Bar, bar, bar, Barb'ra Ann.

Verse 1 (both parts)

Went to a dance, lookin' for romance,
Saw Barb'ra Ann, so I thought I'd take a chance.

Mid-section (both parts sung together)

1 Barb'ra Ann, Barb'ra Ann, Take my hand,
2 Barb'ra Ann, Bar, bar, bar, Barb'ra Ann,

1 O, Barb'ra Ann, Barb'ra Ann, take my hand. You got me rockin' and a rollin',
2 Bar, bar, bar, bar, Barb'ra Ann. You got me rockin' and a rollin',

1 Rockin' and a rollin', Barb'ra Ann, Bar, bar, bar, Barb'ra Ann.
2 Rockin' and a rollin', Barb'ra Ann, Bar, bar, bar, Barb'ra Ann.

Verse 2 (both parts)

Played my fav'rite tune, danced with Betty Lou,
Tried Peggy Sue, but I knew they wouldn't do.

Song format

INTRODUCTION
CHORUS
VERSE 1
MID-SECTION
VERSE 2
MID-SECTION
INTRO
CHORUS

Chord format

Introduction and Chorus

4/4

1 D	2 D	3 D	4 D	Intro
5 D	6 D	7 G	8 G	Chorus
9 D	10 D	11 A7	12 G	
13 D	14 D			

Note: On introduction play first beat of bar only.

Verse

4/4

1 D	2 D	3 D	4 D

Mid-section

4/4

1 G	2 G	3 D	4 D
5 A7	6 G	7 D	8 D

Percussion

18 Project Allundé

Source

I first heard this beautiful traditional East African lullaby in a concert by the group, Sweet Honey in the Rock. This version is adapted from a number of written sources.

Singing style

This must be calm, flowing and melodic, producing a physical rocking in the singers and listeners. Avoid using chordal instruments to accompany.

Teaching the song

In class, work with the chorus, rather than the verse. Learn the piece so that you know it by heart and it becomes part of you. You may need to transpose the piece up to suit your class. All you will need to achieve this is a new starting note. Begin by having the ostinato either sequenced into the computer or played to keep everyone at pitch. If keeping the ostinato going is difficult, a drone note A will work.

Next sing each phrase, getting the pupils to echo back your singing, repeating regular phrases until they are learned. When the class knows all the phrases one group should lead while the rest echo the phrase. Make sure the long notes really last to create the harmony. If you have pupils who can maintain it, add the vocal ostinato. The whole effect is absolutely magical and works very well with a large number.

Performing the song

Performing the verse requires careful planning since the bass ostinato alters. Use the verse for a performance, or special occasion. A group of confident singers takes the melody, whilst the rest in the same parts as before (melody and echo) chant quietly 'Allundé, Allundé'. The verse fits neatly on to the end of the chorus and the bass ostinato at the end of the verse leads back to the chorus.

Follow-up work

1 Pupils can compose music with a similar rhythmic drone, for example, a lullaby or a piece of meditative music.

2 Pupils could compare the effect of *Allundé* with the other lullaby in this pack: the Schubert cradle song (page 60).

18 Project
Allundé

Traditional East African arr. Patrick Allen

18 Project

Allundé

Chorus

Allundé, Allundé, Allundé, Alluya
Allundé, Alluya, Allundé, Alluya

Verse

Je pu a je, je-ku sa
Ai, yai, yai, yé Allundé,
Ai, yai, yai, yé, Ai, yai, yai, yé Allundé

19 Project Michael Finnigan medley

Source

These three partner songs of English and American origin can be sung singly or simultaneously.

A *Skip to my Lou* An American folksong with the style and purpose of a square dance. The song was originally a 'play party game' at a time when some rural communities were barred from conventional dances and instrumental dance tunes for religious reasons.

B *Michael Finnigan* An English traditional song with a similarly dance-based melody.

C *This old man* An English traditional counting song.

Singing style

Skip to my Lou should have all the rhythm and energy of an American square dance, and works best sung with American accents. *Michael Finnigan* is equally rhythmic but the humour of the words is important so pupils should enunciate them clearly.

Teaching the songs

The songs are straightforward, but they should be learned separately by rote and only layered over each other when they are known well.

Performing the songs

The exact format for each song and their combination is entirely up to you and the class. A song can be sung through on its own or the songs can be combined in any number.

Accompanying the songs

Try to get a square dance feel in the style and rhythm of your accompaniment. A strong bass line with off-beat chords will enhance the piece. A bass drum on beats 1 and 3 and light snare on 2 and 4 is both simple and effective.

Follow-up work

1 A square dance is an American country dance, which starts with four couples facing each other in a square. A caller shouts out the steps and moves and a fiddle-band accompanies. What connections between music and dance are pupils aware of? They will perhaps know of social dances, such as square dancing, morris dancing, the waltz, ballroom dancing, live dancing and 'raves'. Pupils could be played various types of dance music and asked to associate them with the appropriate dances, locating the culture and origin of the dance.

2 Aaron Copland's *Rodeo* provides a good link to ballet from the music in this project. He incorporates North American folk dances into a vigorous ballet score.

19 Project

Michael Finnigan medley

Traditional arr. Patrick Allen

19 Project Michael Finnigan medley

19 Project Michael Finnigan medley

Pupil's sheet

Skip to my Lou

(American folksong)

Verse

1 Flies in the buttermilk, two by two, (x 3)
Skip to my Lou, my darling.

Chorus (after each verse)

Lou, Lou, skip to my Lou, (x 3)
Skip to my Lou, my darling.

2 Lost my partner, what'll I do …

3 I'll get another one prettier than you …

4 Flies in the sugar bowl, shoo, fly, shoo …

Michael Finnigan

(English traditional)

1 There was an old man called Michael Finnigan,
He grew whiskers on his chinnigan,
Wind came up and blew them innigan,
Poor old Michael Finnigan (begin again).

2 There was an old man called Michael Finnigan,
He went fishing with a pinnigan,
Caught a fish but dropped it innagan …

3 There was an old man called Michael Finnigan,
He grew fat and then grew thinigan,
Then he died and had to begin again …

This old man

(English traditional)

This old man he played *one*,
He played nick-nack on my *drum*,
With a nick-nack paddy-wack, give a dog a bone,
This old man came rolling home.

Two – shoe
Three – knee
Four – door
Five – hive
Six – sticks
Seven – Heaven
Eight – gate
Nine – line
Ten – hen

Chord format

$\frac{4}{4}$

1	2	3	4
D	A7	D	A7 D

20 Project I-VI-IV-V

Source

The chord sequence I-VI-IV-V is one of the most widespread in popular music and particularly in tunes from the 1950s and 60s. Some of the most famous songs which use it are *All I have to do is dream, Heart and soul* (the theme from *Big*), *Blue moon, Teenager in love, Stand by me, We go together* (from *Grease*), *Stay, Unchained melody, Why do fools fall in love?* and many more. Pupils and their parents might well have some of these songs at home. Which do they know? Could they bring some to class? Pupils could teach the class the melodies and lyrics. Try fitting some of the songs above over the I–VI–IV–V backing.

Singing style

The chord sequence, and the songs, are particularly associated with the 'doo-wop' style of vocal music, which, as well as being melodic, 'polite' and easy on the ear, is characterized by vocal harmonies, vocalized rhythms and skat-style vocal riff backings. This style originated in the 1950s in rhythm 'n' blues singing groups, with 'doo-wop' referring to the kind of backing phrases they used.

Teaching this project

The project begins with held-notes which can be sung over the repeated backing. Introduce these to the class one at a time, allocating each one to a group and slowly layering the harmonies. Skat-style *ostinato* vocalizations are suggested once the notes have been sung to 'Ooh' and 'Aah'. Invent your own as well. There are two alternative accompaniments. **A** is a straightforward 4/4 busking rhythm; **B** divides the beat into triplets to create a 'shuffle' rhythm. Skat vocalizations are suggested for both **B** and **A**.

Once the class can sing the parts over the accompaniment, they have the backing for a number of songs. It is a good idea to begin with some of the group, or yourself, singing the melody to *Heart and soul* over this backing the class are now singing. Most of *Blue moon* will also fit this backing.

Over accompaniment **A** you can sing or play *All I have to do is dream* or *Stand by me*.

All I have to do is dream

(Boudleaux Bryant)

The song was first recorded by the Everly Brothers and is presented in its entirety for a class performance which could involve the vocal backings the pupils have just learned. Remember this is a flexible arrangement and it is unlikely you will use all the elements. The chorus can be divided between two groups of singers. Those with a lower range can sing the first 'Dream' while higher singers can reply with the 'Dream, dream, dream'.

Stand by me

(Ben E. King)

The song was composed by Ben E. King in 1962, in collaboration with Jerry Leiber and Mike Stoller, two celebrated American producers/composers of the early rock era. The song was re-released in the late 1980s and became a number one hit for the second time. This song can be taught in a number of ways:

i as a song for a soloist or small group with the class providing vocal and/or instrumental backing
ii as a song for the whole class to sing with a small group singing the bass riff
iii as a song for the whole class to sing with everyone singing the bass riff as an introduction and coda
iv as an exercise in harmony singing using the vocal backings and bass riff without the main melody
v as an unaccompanied concert piece for skilled singers.

Since the verse and chorus are identical, the backing can easily be programmed into a computer. The song is so widely played in the media that many pupils are familiar with it, although the melody has an improvisatory character which may confuse. The bass riff has an immediate appeal, but the song is difficult to perform well with a group of unconfident singers. It can be effective to teach the melody from the original recording.

Follow-up work

1 Pupils can invent: a) their own backing vocal riffs for the sequence; b) their own melodies, tunes or songs over it.

2 Explain the **'doo-wop'** style to students and play them examples. The terms **riff, ostinato, layered harmony**, **skat** can be explained along with the background to the I–VI–IV–V sequence itself. Get pupils to hear this sequence in songs and to identify when the songs depart from it.

20 Project I-VI-IV-V

arr. Patrick Allen

Harmony 1

Busking patterns

Standard busk

Shuffle busk

Vocalizations using standard busk

Vocalizations using shuffle busk

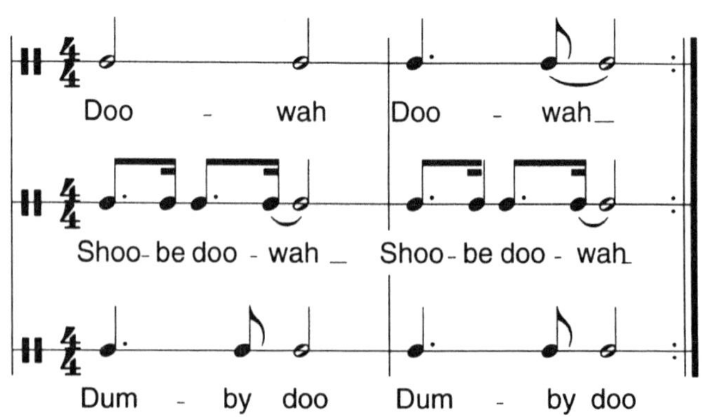

Chord format

4/4 | 1 C Am | 2 F G :|

Skat vocalization: *Heart and soul* (over shuffle busk)

20 Project I-VI-IV-V

All I have to do is dream

Boudleaux Bryant

Use standard busk

20 Project I-VI-IV-V

Pupil's sheet

All I have to do is dream

Boudleaux Bryant

Chorus

Dream, Dream, dream, dream. (x 2)

Verse

1 When I want you in my arms,
When I want you and all your charms,
Whenever I want you all I have to do is …
(Dream)

2 When I feel blue in the night,
And I need you to hold me tight,
Whenever I want you all I have to do is …
(Dream)

3 I need you so, that I could die,
I love you so and that is why,
Whenever I want you all I have to do is …
(Dream)

4 When I want you in my arms,
When I want you and all your charms,
Whenever I want you all I have to do is …
(Dream)

Middle

I can make you mine, taste your lips of wine,
Any time, night or day.
Only trouble is, gee whizz,
I'm dreaming my life away.

Song format

CHORUS
VERSE 1
CHORUS
VERSE 2
LINK TO MIDDLE
MIDDLE
VERSE 3
CHORUS
VERSE 4
CHORUS
FINE (same as link to middle)

Chord format

Chorus

4/4

1	2
C Am	F G :

Verse

4/4

1	2
C Am	F G

(× 3)

Link to middle/Fine

4/4

1	2
C F	C

Middle

4/4

1	2	3	4
F	Em	Dm G	C
5 F	6 Em	7 D	8 G

20 Project I-VI-IV-V

Stand by me

Words: Ben E. King/Music: Jerry Leiber, Mike Stoller

I-VI-IV-V

Pupil's sheet

Stand by me

Words: Ben E. King/Music: Jerry Lieber, Mike Stoller arr. Patrick Allen

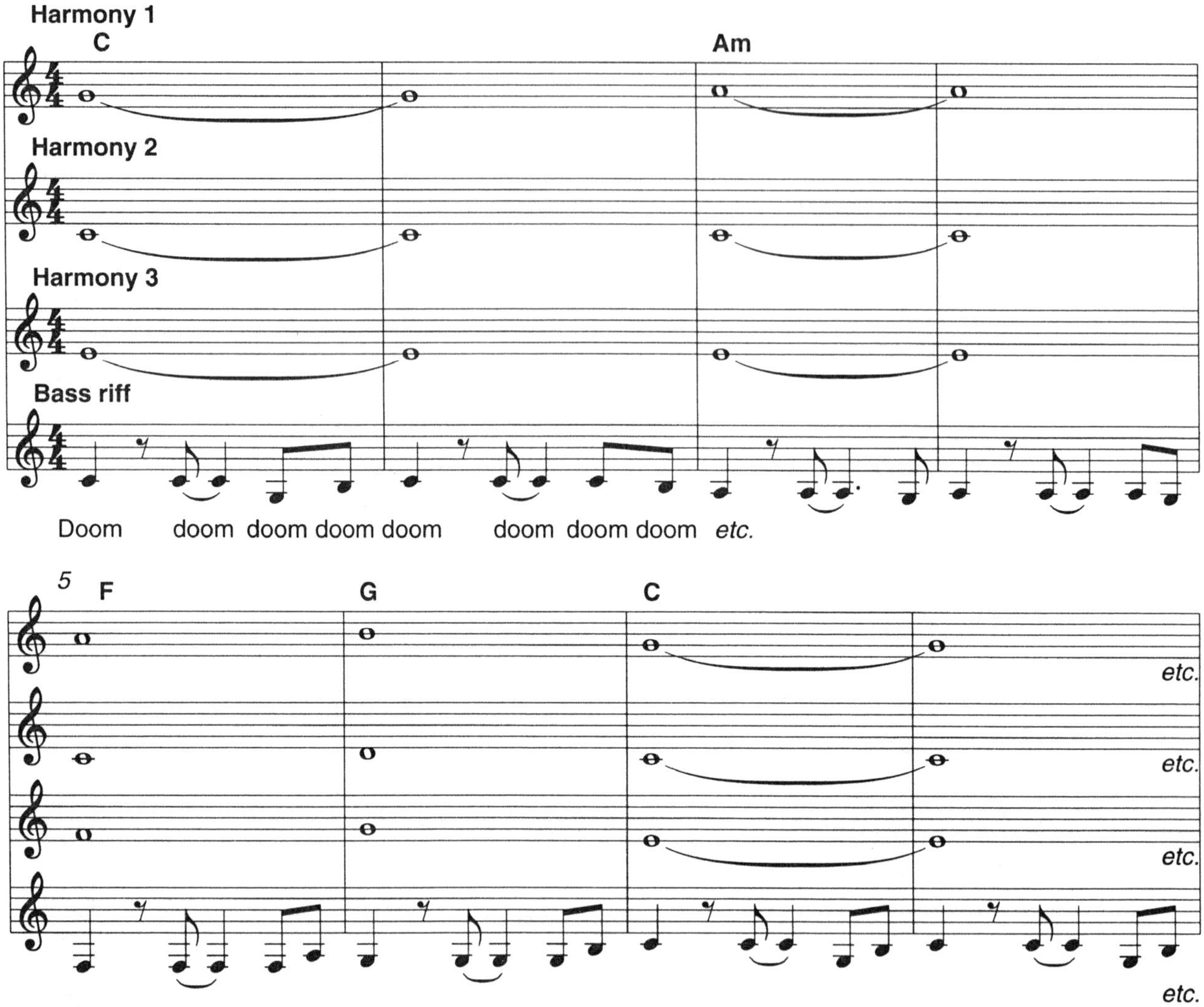

Vocalizations

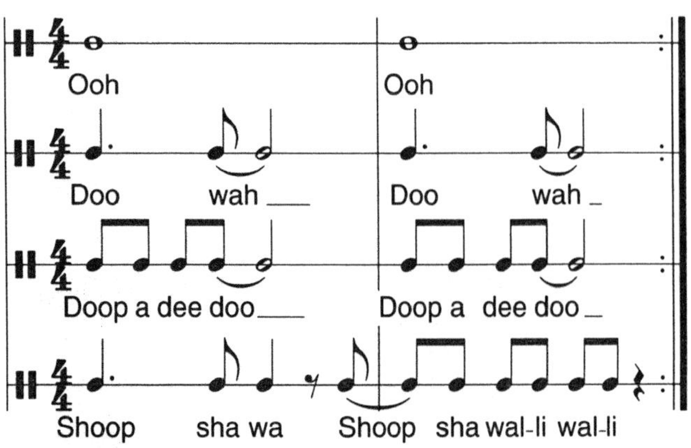

Percussion

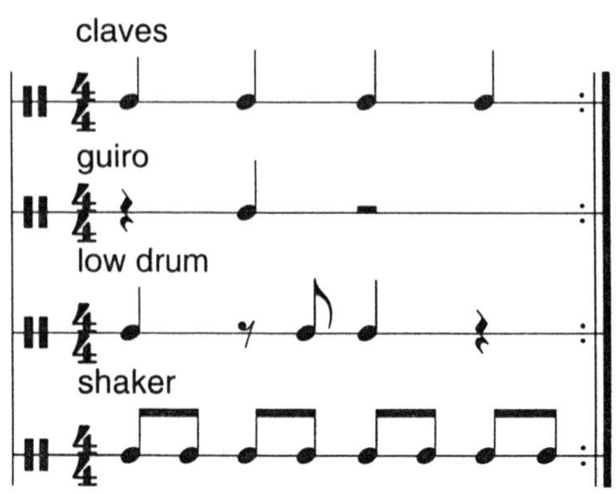

Busking pattern

Chord format

4/4

1 C	2 C	3 Am	4 Am
5 F	6 G	7 C	8 C :

21 *Project* Two Scottish folksongs

Will ye go, lassie, go?

Source

This is a Scottish folksong which is also found in Ireland and England. Several recordings are available by Joan Baez, Judy Collins, the McPeake family and a folk/rock version featured recently in television commercials. It is sometimes known as *Wild mountain thyme*.

Singing style

The long notes must be sustained well and the 'Scotch snaps' and other dotted rhythms should be sung accurately. Many pupils will enjoy this beautiful song, especially if it doesn't drag and the accompaniment is steadily rhythmic and 'busked' in a pop style.

Teaching the song

Everyone should learn the tune, which is best taught with a simple accompaniment. The sung harmony is on one note, D, which can continue all the way through, at any octave. This is quite a good exercise, especially as a way in to learning how to sing a part against the tune.

Performing the song

The chords are simple enough for this to be a whole class instrumental/singing performance.

Loch Lomond

Source

This is a popular Scottish folksong, probably dating from the eighteenth century. It has recently become a rousing Scottish rock anthem since being recorded by the rock/folk group Runrig.

Teaching the song

The song has a straightforward melody and the verse and chorus are almost identical. The class will enjoy it sung with the feeling of a rock or football anthem rather than a twee drawing room ballad. Busking pattern B will encourage this 'feel' for the song.

Follow-up work

1 The single note harmony part in *Will ye go, lassie go* could prompt discussion on the use of the **drone**, particularly in Scottish music, notably on the bagpipes. The use of the backward dotted phrases (Scotch snaps) and the mode could lead on to an exploration of the characteristics of Scottish music. Although the songs use a six-note scale, the **pentatonic scale** should also be discussed, with particular reference to *Auld lang syne* (See 'Social songs' page 167).

2 Much modern popular music uses a drone or pedal bass as a harmonic foundation. Songs by Phil Collins, such as *In the air tonight,* and soul hits by James Brown use a single note foundation.

21 Project
Two Scottish folksongs

Will ye go, lassie, go?

Scottish traditional

21 Project Two Scottish folksongs

Loch Lomond

Scottish traditional arr. Patrick Allen

21 Project Two Scottish folksongs

Pupil's sheet

Will ye go, lassie, go?

Scottish traditional

Verse

1 O, the summertime is coming and the trees are sweetly blooming
And the wild mountain thyme grows around the purple heather.

Chorus (after each verse)

Will ye go, lassie, go? And we'll all go together,
To pluck wild mountain thyme all around the blooming heather.
Will ye go, lassie, go?

2 I will build my love a bower by yon crystal flowing fountain
And on it I will pile all the flowers of the mountain.

3 If my true love will not go, I can surely find another
Where the wild mountain thyme grows around the purple heather.

4 I will build my love a shelter on yon high mountain green
And my love shall be the fairest that the summer sun has seen.

Chord format

Verse

4/4

1 D G	2 D	3 G	4 D
5 G D	6 Bm	7 Em(7)	8 G G/A

Note: When a chord is written thus: G/A the chord of G major is played with A in the bass.

Chorus

4/4

1 D G	2 D	3 G	4 D
5 G D	6 Bm	7 Em(7)	8 G G/A
9 D G	10 D		

Busking pattern

Note: Adapt the pattern to the chord changes.

21 Project Two Scottish folksongs

Pupil's sheet

Loch Lomond

Scottish traditional

Chorus (after each verse)

O, you'll take the high road and I'll take the low,
And I'll be in Scotland before you,
But me and my true love will never meet again,
On the bonnie, bonnie banks of Loch Lomond.

Verse

1 By yon bonnie banks and by yon bonnie braes,
Where the sun shines bright on Loch Lomond,
Where me and my true love were ever wont to go,
On the bonnie, bonnie banks of Loch Lomond.

2 I mind where we parted in yon shady glen,
On the steep, steep side of Ben Lomond,
In deep purple hues all the highland hills we viewed,
And the moon coming out in the gloaming.

3 The small birds do sing and the wild flowers spring,
And in sunshine the waters are sleeping,
The poor broken heart will not see a second spring,
And the world does not know how we're greeting.

Busking patterns

A

B

Chord format

Verse

4/4

1 D Bm	2 G A	3 D Bm	4 G D
5 G Bm	6 Em G A	7 D Bm	8 Em A D

Chorus

4/4

1 D Bm	2 G A	3 D Bm	4 G D
5 G Bm	6 Em G A	7 D Bm	8 Em A D

22 Project Two Renaissance songs

This project looks at two Renaissance songs based on dance tunes and adapted for school use.

Pavane

(Arbeau)

Source

This pavane from the *Orchésographie* in Langres dates from 1589 and has been reharmonized for this project. The melody is the alto part. The *Orchésographie* was a treatise on dancing by Thoinot Arbeau and is an important source of information on Renaissance dances as well as the music of the period.

Singing style

The piece uses a narrow range of notes which should be given their full value and well pitched. Although a pavane is a slow dance it must not drag.

Teaching the song

This can be learned for instruments and voices in any combination and is an ideal opportunity for instruments to double voices. The melody and soprano parts are direct parallels (apart from a suspension in bar 4) and can be easily learned. In this piece it is best if the students see the music, perhaps using it as a reading exercise.

Performing the song

Ideally a variety of singers and players would learn all four parts to create a flexible performance where instruments and voices are combined in a variety of ways. The students themselves can choose how the performance should unfold. The percussion is an important element.

Follow-up work

1 Pupils should decide upon the performance structure of the piece. This can then be tape-recorded for evaluation.

2 Pupils could learn more about the pavane (and the accompanying, faster, galliard) and hear recordings of Renaissance dances (Philip Pickett's recording of *Tylman Susato Dansereye 1551* is recommended). Pupils could identify **tempo, instrumentation, dynamics** and basic rhythmic features.

3 Pupils could listen to *The Capriol Suite* by Peter Warlock, which uses this and other dances from the *Orchésographie* in an appealing orchestral adaptation.

Santa Maria

Source

This is an anonymous Portuguese Renaissance dance, of popular origin.

Singing style

This energetic and rhythmic piece can be very exciting when it works. Many classes will find this hard, so it may serve as an extension activity for more able students.

Teaching the song

This is a more difficult piece, which can stand or fall on an understanding of the 6/8 3/4 combination so important in much Spanish and Portuguese music. It is important that pupils fully feel and understand the rhythm before attempting this. It might be best to programme the rhythm into the computer/sequencer first, and perhaps use this to drive the music in the early stages. Once the rhythm is secure the song comes quite easily. The ostinato is simple and can be at any octave. It can be instrumental or vocal and could become part of your computer/sequenced backing. The descant part is also not difficult and can be sung easily. Once all the parts are running this is a most infectious piece, and works best combining voices and instruments.

Performing the song

This, and the pavane, would make good concert pieces in any combination of voices and instruments – and with plenty of percussion.

Follow-up work

The rhythm used in this piece is also widely heard in Latin American music as a result of Spanish and Portuguese colonization. The best known example is *America* from *West side story* by Leonard Bernstein, modelled on Puerto Rican dance rhythms. Pupils could compare the two pieces.

22 Project Two Renaissance songs

Pupil's sheet

Pavane

Arbeau (1589) arr. Patrick Allen

**Note: The note G in bar 4 in the soprano part, which creates an effective suspension, can be replaced with the note A if desired.*

22 Project Two Renaissance songs

Pupil's sheet

Pavane

Arbeau (1589)

1 Smooth as the deepest stream,
Fairer than the sweetest dream, (repeat)
Thy looks have made me blind,
Love rages in my mind. (repeat)

2 My choice would be again,
Light with dark, this joy with pain, (repeat)
Thy beauty fills my life,
Peace, war and loving strife. (repeat)

Chord format

4/4

1	2	3	4
Dm A	Dm C F	F Gm F/A	Gm7 C F
5	**6**	**7**	**8**
F C	Dm A	F G Dm	Dm A Dm

Note: When a chord is written thus: F/A the chord of F major is played with an A in the bass.

Percussion

22 Project Two Renaissance songs

Pupil's sheet

Santa Maria

Portugese arr. Patrick Allen

22 Project Two Renaissance songs

Pupil's sheet

Santa Maria

Portugese

1 Let us build up the flaming fire,
Let us raise up our glasses higher!
Let us stamp our feet, bells are ringing,
Join the carnival, dancing and singing.

2 Now forget all the cares of living,
Greet our friends, all our foes forgiving.
Let us stamp our feet, bells are ringing,
Join the carnival, dancing and singing.

Descant

Carnival pleasures, carnival time,
Drink by the measure, let's forget time.

Chord format

(6/8) 3/4

1 Am	2 Em	3 Em	4 Am
5 Am	6 Em	7 Em	8 Am

Percussion

23 Project You are not alone

Source

The beautiful song in this project, *You are not alone* by R. Kelly, was a number one hit for Michael Jackson in 1995 and can be found, along with other material suitable for classroom use, on his *History* album. The songwriter, R. Kelly, is an excellent performer in his own right.

Singing style

The song requires a smooth, melodic delivery, well sustained notes and quite long breaths. The vocal range is a comfortable one for this age group, but they should make an effort to support the notes properly.

Teaching the song

Most pupils seem to know this song, but it's best to play the melody clearly while in the learning stages. Teach the song in sections, and then 'glue' the bits together. The harmony part is based on the recording and can be added quite easily once the chorus is known by the class. If pupils are given a copy of this section of the score they can 'read' their part.

Accompanying the song

Piano: This part is written out in full since the accompaniment style varies and some of the chords are quite complex. Use this once the pupils are confident with the song.

Busking/Chord parts: The verse and chorus are written as simple chord sequences (the 7ths can be ignored if pupils are playing triads). The chords are played to a simple crotchet pulse. The bridge passages and verse middle have more complex chords, so pupils may wish to play single notes in these sections. These sections are written both as chords and as the individual notes of the chord. Pupils will then play note 1, 2, 3 or 4 of the chord.

Follow-up work

1 There is scope for solo singing if the verses are divided between members of the class.

2 R. Kelly is a successful black American songwriter and Michael Jackson is one of the world's greatest pop performers. The class could consider the impact of black Americans on popular music from soul and gospel and early Tamla Motown to the rap and swing performers of the 1990s. Michael Jackson's career, its tabloid moments aside, is a history of modern black American music in itself. The pupils themselves are often a valuable source of information and recordings of this music and can be relied on for information on the most up-to-date styles and artists. *The Oxford Companion to Popular Music* provides excellent summaries of most of these styles.

23 Project You are not alone

R. Kelly arr. Patrick Allen

23 Project You are not alone

23 Project You are not alone

23 Project You are not alone

Pupil's sheet

R. Kelly

23 Project You are not alone

R. Kelly

Verse

1 Another day has gone, I'm still all alone.
How could this be? You're not here with me.
You never said goodbye. Someone tell me why –
Did you have to go and leave my world so cold?

Verse middle

Every day I sit and ask myself, how did love slip away?
Someone whispers in my ear and says:

Chorus (after each verse middle)

You are not alone, I am here with you.
Though you're far away, I am here to stay.
But you are not alone, I am here with you,
Though we're far apart, you're always in my heart –
You are not alone.

Verse

2 Just the other night I thought I heard you cry,
Asking me to come and hold you in my arms.
I can hear your prayers, your burdens I will bear,
But first I need your hand that forever can begin.

Vocal bridge

Whisper three words and I'll come running,
And girl/boy you know that I'll be there.

Song format

VERSE 1 } 1
VERSE MIDDLE } 1
CHORUS
INST. BRIDGE
VERSE 2 } 2
VERSE MIDDLE } 2
CHORUS
VOCAL BRIDGE
CHORUS x 2

Chord format

Verse

4/4	1 C	2 Am	3 Dm7	4 G
	5 C	6 Am	7 Dm7	8 G

Verse middle

3	G E	A	C	D	Single notes of chor
2	D C#	F	A	B	
1	B♭ A	D	F	G	
3/2	1 Gm/B♭A	2 Dm	3 F	4 G	Chord

Note: When a chord is written thus: Gm/B♭ the chord of G minor is played with a B♭ in the bass.

Chorus

4/4	1 C	2 Am	3 Dm7	4 G	
	5 C	6 Am	7 Dm7	8 G	9 C

Instrumental bridge

(4)	(F)		(F)		Single notes of chorc
3	E♭ D	G	E♭ D	D	
2	C B♭	E	C B♭	B	
1	A♭ G	C	A♭ G	G	
4/4	1 A♭ Gm7	2 C	3 A♭ Gm7	4 G	Chord

Vocal bridge

(4)	(F)	(E♭)	(F)		Single notes of chorc
3	E♭ D	C	E♭ D	D	
2	C B♭	A♭	C B♭	B	
1	A♭ G	F	A♭ G	G	
4/4	1 A♭ Gm7	2 Fm7	3 A♭ Gm7	4 G	Chord

Coda

4/4	1 C

24 Project Slavonska poskocika

Source

This traditional Croatian song was originally transcribed from the singing of Lado by Larry Gordon and appears in Mary Cay Brass's *Village Harmony – Traditional Songs of the Balkans*.

Singing style

A rousing drinking song, this can be sung with real gusto. Croatian singing has a spirited, forward sound which comes easily to many teenagers, but needs to remain musical and tuneful at all times.

Teaching the song

This is an easy and fun song, but the full arrangement makes it look harder than it really is. The pupil's sheet reduces the song to its simplest form. An eight-bar verse and a four-bar chorus which is sung four times.

Please treat the verse flexibly to suit your class. It can be sung in unison or in harmony, in any octave and parts A and B are entirely interchangeable at any point. For example, in a class where the low singers outnumber the high swap parts A and B for the first four bars of the verse, having group B singing the 'melody' an octave lower while group A sing group B's harmony part. For the second half of the verse parts A and B sing as written. With groups who find harmony difficult just sing the first half of A twice and that becomes the verse. Be flexible. This is a folk art, not tablets of stone.

The chorus looks daunting, but is easy. It can be sung in the following ways:

i main tune only (in any octave)
ii main tune plus one or more of the canonic/imitative harmonies. Once they have their starting note, each part should come in easily.

Part A is the main tune with a harmony in parallel thirds.
Part A div. is directly canonic.
Part B is a parallel harmony and starts a fifth below the melody.

Performing the song

Start the first section at a steady *moderato* and gradually speed it up. By the time you reach the end of the chorus it should be going as fast as you can manage! The chorus is very exciting with all the simple, rhythmic canonic entries. The last bar should be sung with a real *marcato*. The chords are easy and a small Balkan band can be created using a string bases, an accordion sound for the off-beat chords and piano with flutes or clarinets playing the various melodies. Why not have instruments leading each group of singers?

A note on pronunciation: ***drma*** is pronounced *durma*; *zica* pronounced ***tsika***; ***kabanica*** pronounced *kabanitscha*.

Follow-up work

1 Play the class more music from the Balkans, particularly recordings of the *Mystère des voix bulgares* from Disques Cellier, volume 2 CAD 801 CD is particularly good. Note the strident vocal tone, the eerie harmonies and the relish of dissonance. How unlike our western ideals of vocal skill and success. There is a recording of *Slavonska poskocika* on the CD *Village harmony, traditional songs of the Balkans* from the Northern Harmony Publishing Company, Plainfield, Vermont, USA.

2 The pupils should be aware of the *accelerando* in this piece. What is the effect on singers and listeners?

3 What other **social songs** do the pupils know, which encourage friendship and fun? What occasions do we use them and what sort of songs should they be? They will probably mention ones like the *Hokey Cokey, Agadoo* and *The birdie song*. See also page 164.

24 Project Slavonska poskocika

Croatian traditional arr. Patrick Allen

Full harmony version
Verse

24 Project Slavonska poskocika

24 Project Slavonska poskocika

24 Project Slavonska poskocika

Pupil's sheet

Croatian traditional arr. Patrick Allen

Verse

1 Let us sing and raise our glass to heaven.
Life is short, let music fill our hearts. (x 2)

Chorus

Op zica, zica, zica, drma mise kabanica! (x 3)
Op zica, zica, zica, drma mise kabanic!

2 Play a tune to set the room a-dancing.
Sing and dance, let music fill our hearts. (x 2)

3 Love and live and play the tune with feeling.
One more time, let music fill our hearts. (x 2)

Chord format

Verse

2/4

1 G D	2 G D	3 G D	4 G
5 G D	6 G D	7 G D	8 G :

Chorus

2/4

1 D	2 A7	3 D	4 A7
5 D	6 A7	7 D	8 A :

25 Project Siyahamba

Source

This traditional Zulu chant can be heard in a number of arrangements, and is sometimes called *Walking in the light*. It has become popular with young choirs through a three-part setting by Doreen Rao.

Singing style

The tempo must be steady, but the rhythmic feel should be relaxed. with pupils clapping or swaying in time.

Teaching the song

At its simplest, just the melody with chords and percussion will work. The two chanted harmony parts are written in the bass clef, but the bass part itself can be sung at any octave. These parts are simple and the whole class could have a go at them over the chordal backing. The harmony part which follows the main melody at intervals of 3rds and 4ths is more difficult. The lower chanting parts are really very effective against the tune, but any combination of the parts will work.

Follow-up work

1 Try composing words which are relevant to your school, class or town, or collective beliefs.

2 Pupils could listen to the version of this recorded by the African Children's Choir, *Walking in the light*, Alliance Music.

25 Project Siyahamba

Zulu traditional arr. Patrick Allen

Note: For variety the words of the backing chant can change with the verse to 'We are walking', 'We are running' etc.

25 Project Siyahamba

Zulu traditional

Verse

1 Siyahamb'e kukhanyeni kwenkhos (x 4)
Siyahamba, Siyahamba, Siyahamb'e
kukhanyeni kwenkhos. (x 2)

2 We are walking to where freedom begins, (x 4)
We are walking, we are walking,
We are walking to where freedom begins. (x 2)

3 We are running to where justice begins, (x 4)
We are running …

4 We are marching to where weapons
are gone, (x 4)
We are marching …

5 We are sailing to where waters are calm, (x 4)
We are sailing …

6 We are flying to our heaven on earth, (x 4)
We are flying …

Chord format

4/4

1 G	2 G	3 D	4 G :
5 C	6 G	7 D	8 G :

Coda

4/4

1 G

Percussion

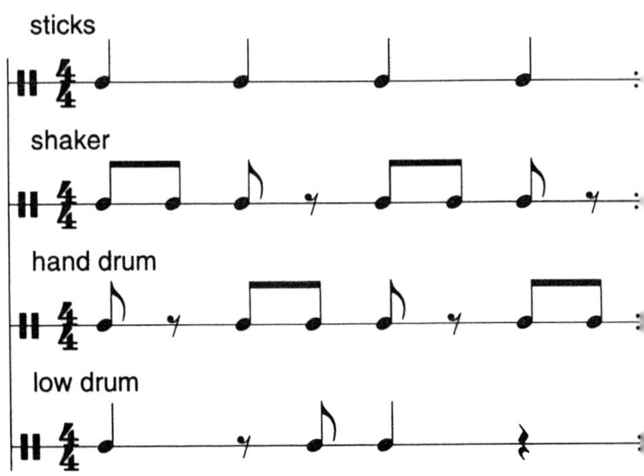

26 Project Two classics

Source

A Theme from *Rondo, Sonatina in G* (Op. 36 no. 5) by Muzio Clementi (1752–1832) This well-known melody, adapted for a famous pop song, is rarely attributed to its true composer. Clementi was a celebrated pianist and composer, who was born an Italian and died an Englishman.

B The *Ode to joy* theme from the *Ninth Symphony* by Ludwig van Beethoven (1770–1827) This choral theme from the last movement of the symphony (1824), was a setting of Schiller's poem 'An die Freude'. The simple, but majestic melody sets Schiller's view of an idealized humanity.

Singing style

These pieces will survive most types of musical setting, from 'authentic' to pop and rock. Choose an approach which suits you and the class.

Teaching the songs

Clementi: Many pupils will recognize this melody and it works well to give it a slightly pop treatment when first learning it. The words provided are entirely optional, so use others if you prefer. This is a simple, gentle step-wise melody which can be learned easily. Many pupils may also wish to learn it as a keyboard piece.

Beethoven: Another well-known tune, which some pupils may have learned as a keyboard or instrumental piece. This was written for the voice, however, and pupils should have the experience of singing it. There is a tendency to sing this in a plodding, slightly *staccato* manner, so try to make the students sing it *legato*. A pop setting of this may appeal initially.

Follow-up work

1 Introduce the pupils to the original pieces from which these songs come. The Clementi is widely available and mercifully easy to play. The pupils really appreciate a performance by their teacher! The concepts of **sonata** and **rondo** form are very well illustrated by this piece. How many times does the theme re-appear? Is it the same each time it returns? How many different tunes are there between each restatement of the theme?

2 Clementi was alive at the transition from harpsichord to piano. This piece provides a wonderful opportunity to explain the revolution the piano represented.

3 The Beethoven provides an excellent opportunity to introduce the concepts of **symphony** and **symphonic orchestra**, as well as the principal components of choral music: **recitative, chorus, aria, duet, trio** etc. Pupils will be fascinated by the drama of this movement and the various settings and arrangements of the theme they have sung.

4 Find a variety of ways to accompany these melodies, to show how the same chords can transform the character of the piece depending on how they are played. Pupils could make up their own backings for the melodies in groups, using the given chords.

26 Project Two classics

Pupil's sheet

Theme from Rondo/Dove of peace

Clementi/Words: Patrick Allen

1 Tell me can you see, flying there so free,
Far above the world with its wings unfurled?
Soaring in the air, higher than we dare,
Everybody simply turns away.
Hearts which search for love,
Look into the sky,
See the dove of peace fly by.

2 Tell me can you hear, what there is to fear?
Can you tell me why white wings pass us by?
Soaring in the air, we don't seem to care,
Everybody simply turns away.
Fill your heart with love,
Reach out with your hand,
And the dove of peace will land.

Busking pattern

Held chords or simple arpeggios over

Piano bass

etc.

Chord format

4/4

1 G	2 C	3 G	4 C
5 G	6 Dm	7 Em	8 F
9 G	10 C	11 G	12 C

Percussion

27 Project

Two classics

Pupil's sheet

Ode to joy/Euro anthem

Beethoven/Words: Patrick Allen

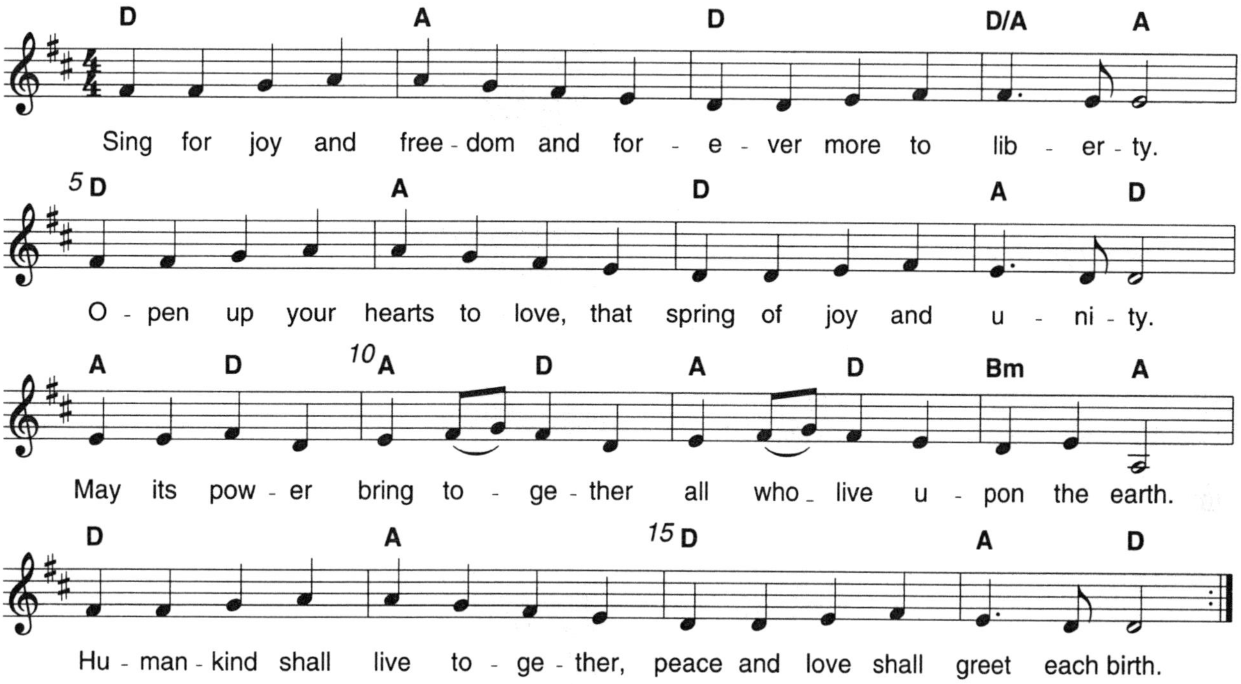

1 Sing for joy and freedom and forever more to liberty.
Open up your hearts to love, that spring of joy and unity.
May its power bring together all who live upon the earth.
Humankind shall live together, peace and love shall greet each birth.

2 May the joy that fills our hearts blow far across the stormy sea.
May the very air we breathe be filled with gentle purity.
In the sky and on the land sing this bright song of liberty,
May our children play in freedom, teaching us how life should be.

Chord format

4/4

1 D	2 A	3 D	4 D/A A	5 D	6 A	7 D	8 A D
9 A D	10 A D	11 A D	12 Bm A	13 D	14 A	15 D	16 A D

Busking pattern

Percussion

Note: When a chord is written thus: D/A the chord of D major is played with A in the bass.

27 Project No hiding place

Source

This is a North American spiritual which has been re-arranged and adapted for easy harmony singing and flexible use.

Singing style

Rhythmic, relaxed gospel style.

Teaching the song

The instrumental backing is an ostinato which runs through the whole song. If you sequence this into your computer you will find it easy to teach the song and the harmonies. The melody is in the middle part, but all the harmony parts work equally well as a main melody. All the parts can be sung at any octave and the song will work with any number of parts. The lowest part works particularly well an octave higher. Begin by teaching the song in unison, using a call and response technique. You should sing the phrase (usually two bars, then four) and then the class immediately echoes it. In this way the whole song can be taught aurally.

The harmonies are so natural and close to the melody, that providing you have chosen the right voices for each part, they will happen very easily, once pupils have their starting notes. Keep repeating lines and phrases until pupils are confident with the words, rhythms and pitches.

Performing the song

Perform the song in a way that suits your group. You will need to adapt the score to fit your chosen format for the song. For example, the chorus could be used alone as a way of teaching parallel harmony singing. It can work with a class, a choir or an assembly sized group. You might try the following suggestions:

i unison, two-part harmony or three-part harmony throughout

ii call and response – the verses (and chorus) are sung by a soloist (or small group) before the whole group repeat them

iii singing the verses cumulatively. The format would be:
Chorus (x 2);
Verse 1, Chorus;
Verses 1, 2, Chorus;
Verses 1, 2, 3, Chorus (x 2).

Accompanying the song

The singers should clap the off-beat, which will physically involve them in the piece. The song can be accompanied by piano, guitar, a small instrumental ensemble or sequenced computer. A vocal bass line ostinato is also included in the arrangement.

Follow-up work

Gospel music should be discussed and heard. The influence of African music and the spiritual uplift generated by years of oppression and slavery produced a style very different from the European hymn singing from which it developed. What differences do the pupils notice in singing style and delivery? Discuss the vocal delivery which is **strong** and **rhythmic**, **improvisatory**, full of **portamentos**, **grace notes** and **syncopations**. The tradition is communal and participatory with high emotional levels and often relies on **call and response**, with a chorus responding in **parallel harmony** to a lead singer.

Gospel, soul and modern pop styles are very closely linked. Can the class see similarities? A singer such as Aretha Franklin bridges the genres and links the styles.

27 *Project*

No hiding place

North American spiritual arr. Patrick Allen

27 Project No hiding place

Note: Omit final rest of verse if continuing immediately to next verse.

27 Project No hiding place

Pupil's sheet

North American spiritual

Chorus

You can't hide away from that judgement day,
There's no hiding place down there.

Verse

1 Oh, I went to the rock to hide my face,
The rock cried out: 'No hiding place!'

2 Oh, the rock cried out: 'I'm burnin' too,
I wanna go to heaven as well as you!'

3 Oh, the sinner man gambled, he gambled and fell,
He wanna go to heaven, but he had to go to hell.

Song format 1

CHORUS (x 2)
VERSE 1
CHORUS
VERSE 2
CHORUS
VERSE 3
CHORUS (x 2)

Song format 2

CHORUS (x 2)
VERSE 1
CHORUS
VERSE 1
VERSE 2
CHORUS
VERSE 1
VERSE 2
VERSE 3
CHORUS (x 2)

Chord format

Chords	$\frac{4}{4}$	1 D Em7	2 D Em7 :
Bass line	$\frac{4}{4}$	3 D A	4 D A :

Vocal ostinato bass line

Percussion

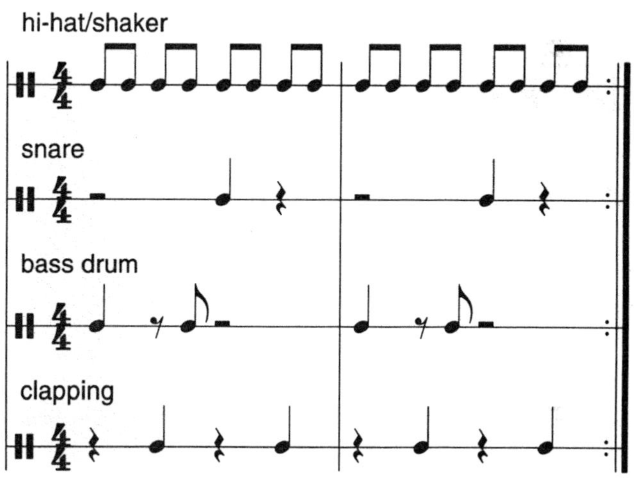

Busking pattern

28 Project Babethandaza

Source

This is a traditional South African song, which has a large number of variants.

Singing style

The song should be sung with a free, relaxed and rhythmic singing style, with scope for portamentos and grace notes. However, do not compromise on the rhythm and syncopations, which are essential to the appeal of the piece. Take time to really get to know and feel the rhythm of this infectious piece yourself before you take it to the class. Although the syncopations look difficult they will seem perfectly natural to the pupils once you are confident with them yourself.

Teaching the song

The song should be learnt aurally. Recite the words with the rhythm of the melody, getting the class to chant back, first individual words and small sections and then the whole song. Enjoy the words. There aren't many of them and they are fun to say. Keep a steady crotchet beat behind your syncopated chanting, either marking time yourself, or using a drum machine or computer to keep the beat. If all of the suggested percussion patterns are programmed they will really lift your rehearsal.

Now teach the melody itself in small sections. Have the whole class sing the melody, in whatever octave is appropriate. When both sections of the melody are secure, the first harmony (soprano) can be added. This is such a direct parallel of the melody the pupils should lock into it easily. Don't leave anyone idle – they could all sing it, or you could divide the class immediately into parts. Feel free to prompt with instruments, but try to aim for unaccompanied performing. Since this is by origin an unaccompanied piece, the given chords are an approximation, but could prove helpful to keep everyone in pitch. Be sure to keep a D in the bass when you play the Em chord.

A note on pronunciation: the vowels should be pure and well rounded and the pupils can be encouraged to really move their mouths. ***nje*** is pronounced ***(n)je***, with the emphasis on the 'j' (the 'n' can be almost silent); ***ngemi*** is pronounced ***ungemi***; ***-th-*** pronounced ***-t-***; ***bagudala*** pronounced ***bagoodala***.

Performing the song

The song will work in unison or with any of the additional harmonies. Always use percussion or clapping.

Percussion can be added as the piece progresses, but the syncopations on the bass drum and cow bell are not easy, so don't let the piece be ruined for the sake of them. It's worth using the computer to keep the rhythm going at this stage. Pupils could all clap the crotchet pulse or the off-beat.

If the pupils forget the harmony you have taught them, but make up their own, don't stop them (providing it fits)! This piece works best without tuned instruments, although the chords, or bass line could be included for added security.

Follow-up work

1 If the piece has gone well try to add the third harmony (tenor) which also fits very easily once the melody is known.

2 The bass part uses only two notes which could be played on an instrument or sung if there are boys with changed voices in the class. It is ideal for a concert performance or an assembly, where adults or older pupils could support.

3 This makes an excellent concert piece. It can start with the melody on its own with a crotchet pulse behind, adding parts one at a time until everyone is singing. Percussion parts can also be entered cumulatively. Remain in the *Sin nje* section while you are adding parts and move to the *Oo mama* section once everyone is singing and playing. It can end by having parts drop out one by one, leaving just the melody.

28 Project Babethandaza

South African traditional arr. Patrick Allen

Sin nje nje nje ngemi thandazo (x 2)
Ngemi thandazo, ngemi thandazo (x 2)
Oo mama bagudala, Babethandaza (x 2)
Babethandaza, Babethandaza (x 2)

Chord format

4/4

1 D	2 A7 D	3 D	4 A7 D
5 Em/D D	6 A7 D	7 Em/D D	8 A7 D :

Note: When a chord is written thus: Em/D the chord of E minor is played with D in the bass.

Percussion

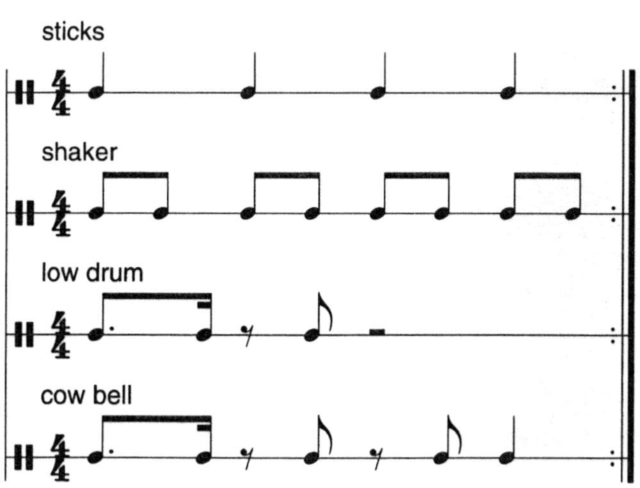

28 Project Babethandaza

South African traditional arr. Patrick Allen

Three-part arrangement (Melody in alto)

28 Project

Babethandaza

South African traditional arr. Patrick Allen

29 Project Down in the valley

Source

Down in the valley is an American children's song from the African–American oral tradition, originally accompanied by a range of hand movements.

Singing style

The song should be sung in a free and relaxed manner with the singers feeling the infectious rhythm, perhaps by clapping the off-beat.

Teaching the song

This simple song is presented in a number of ways and teachers should choose those parts and arrangements which will best suit their class and the individuals within it. It can be taught as a unison song with chordal accompaniment; with vocal ostinati backings or as a parallel harmony arrangement. The full four-part arrangement may only be suitable in an extra-curricular context. The song will work with just the main tune, hand clapping and simple chords, or even unaccompanied.

The song should be taught by rote. It is so short that this can be done in one go with the pupils joining in as they learn it.

Once the main melody is learned, teach the whole class the vocal ostinati as a separate activity. Like the melody, they can be sung in any octave. Once these are learned the ostinati and the song can run simultaneously. The most important ostinati are parts one and two and it should be possible to have these two, plus the melody, running at the same time quite quickly, once the group is divided.

The full four-part arrangement of the song would suit a concert performance. The harmonies are entirely natural, following the contours of the melody, whilst fitting into the harmonic framework. To teach the alto part *either* teach it to the whole class and then divide *or* leave the melody singers running while you lead a group through the part. The tenor part can be pitched above the melody if you have no singers in the correct range. The bass part is very easy and can be sung (or played) in any octave.

Follow-up work

Both this piece and *Babethandaza* (see page 134) are an excellent introduction to **four-part harmony singing**. If you want to start a four-part choir in your school, choose the best singers you have observed in class and bring them together to sing this song and *Babethandaza*. Make it fun and rhythmic. You don't even have to call the gathering a 'choir' if the word has negative connotations for them. (I call our informal gatherings 'Power Singing'!) The bass lines are very easy in both and even boys with recently changed voices will manage them.

29 Project Down in the valley

North American traditional arr. Patrick Allen

29 Project

Down in the valley

North American traditional arr. Patrick Allen

Four-part parallel harmony version

29 Project Down in the valley

Pupil's sheet

North American traditional

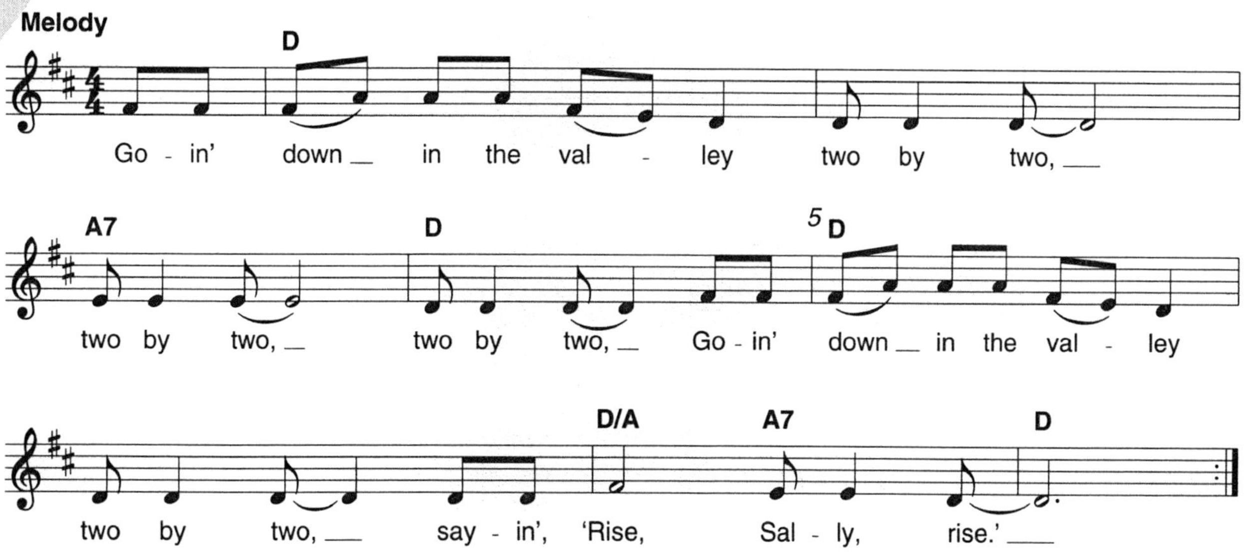

1 Goin' down in the valley two by two, two by two, two by two,
Goin' down in the valley two by two, sayin', 'Rise Sally, rise.'

2 Let me see you make a motion …

3 Won't you come and join together …

4 Come and raise your hands to heaven …

5 Goin' down in the valley …

Chord format

4/4

1 D	2 D	3 A7	4 D
5 D	6 D	7 D/A A7	8 D

Note: When a chord is written thus: D/A the chord of D major is played with A in the bass.

Coda

4/4

1 D

Busking patterns

Percussion

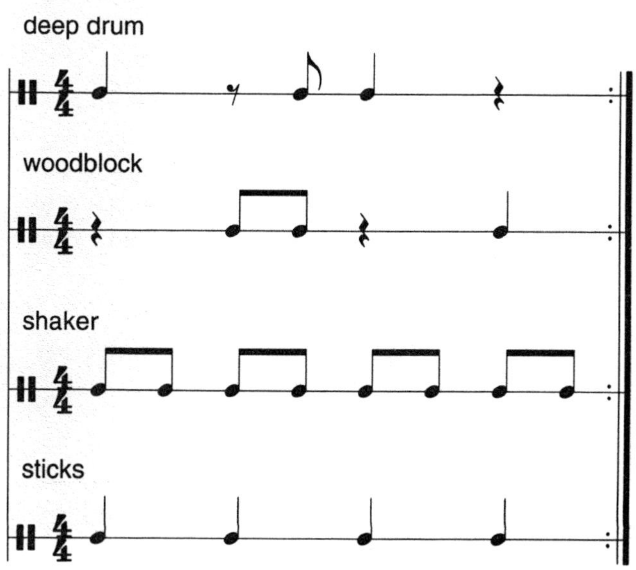

30 Project Layers

This project contains five songs, all constructed on a principle of layering simple melodic ideas, to produce complex sounding pieces. The backings keep running in a continuous loop and the pieces are repeated as often as you like. The songs work with as many parts as your class can manage. They encourage independent part-singing and encourage pupils to concentrate on both their own part and what is going on around them. Some, in their fullest form, may be too difficult for a class, but may be suitable for a large group, an assembly or a performance.

Source

Tina singu is based on a song from Lesotho; all the others in this project have been newly composed over familiar chord progressions.

Teaching the songs

A *Keep moving forward:* This is a round in four parts working over the chord sequence D, Bm, Em, A. It should be taught as a continuous melody to the whole class, with the chord sequence running behind, preferably programmed into the computer. Once the pupils are confident with the melody it can be sung with canonic entries with the class in halves, then thirds and, if they can manage it, in quarters.

B *The fourth circle:* Based on the circle of fourths, this piece uses three simple sequential phrases which rhythmically complement each other. Divide the group according to vocal range and teach each group one of the melodic phrases, layering up the piece as you go. An exceptional group could manage this piece as a round.

C *Tina singu:* Each line of this song can be allocated to a group within the class, selected according to vocal range. The groups singing Parts 1 and 2 can learn each other's parts and swap, as in a round, but the group singing Part 3 should stick with their more difficult part. The backing should keep running all the time you are teaching the song.

D *Freedom highway:* This is based on one of the layered melodic ostinati in the introduction (see page 18), is very simple to learn and works well unaccompanied. Set the ostinati running first, but reserve some of your more confident singers for the melody. Although the melody is not difficult it might be worth going over it with this group separately. An optional descant is provided.

E *Hymn for the earth:* This is a compelling chord sequence with four layered ostinato phrases, of which the fourth is the least important. Over this the stately 'hymn' tune can be sung by a group of confident singers. In its full form this will work best with a large gathering or a group of selected singers.

Follow-up work

1 When a round is presented vertically, as in *Keep moving forward*, it is easier to see how they are constructed, being made of phrases which harmonize with each other. This piece could form the basis of an explanation of rounds and canons to the class.

2 Pupils can be given opportunities to layer complementary melodic ostinati either using a simple modal scale (pentatonic or dorian) or a simple chord sequence such as that in *Freedom highway* or *Keep moving forward*.

3 There is an opportunity here to introduce pupils to the style of Baroque choral music. Apart from using the circle of fourths so familiar in Baroque music, *The fourth circle* also uses melodically independent settings of the words in each part, similar to that used in choral music of the period. If pupils are able to follow a score of any section of Handel's *Messiah*, they will see a similar treatment of text.

4 These chord sequences could be used to develop the pupils' own layered compositions for classes.

30 Project Layers

Keep moving forward

Traditional arr. Patrick Allen/Words: Patrick Allen

30 Project Layers

The fourth circle

Patrick Allen

30 Project Layers

Tina singu

Lesotho arr. Patrick Allen

30 Project Layers

Freedom highway

Patrick Allen

30 Project Layers

Freedom highway

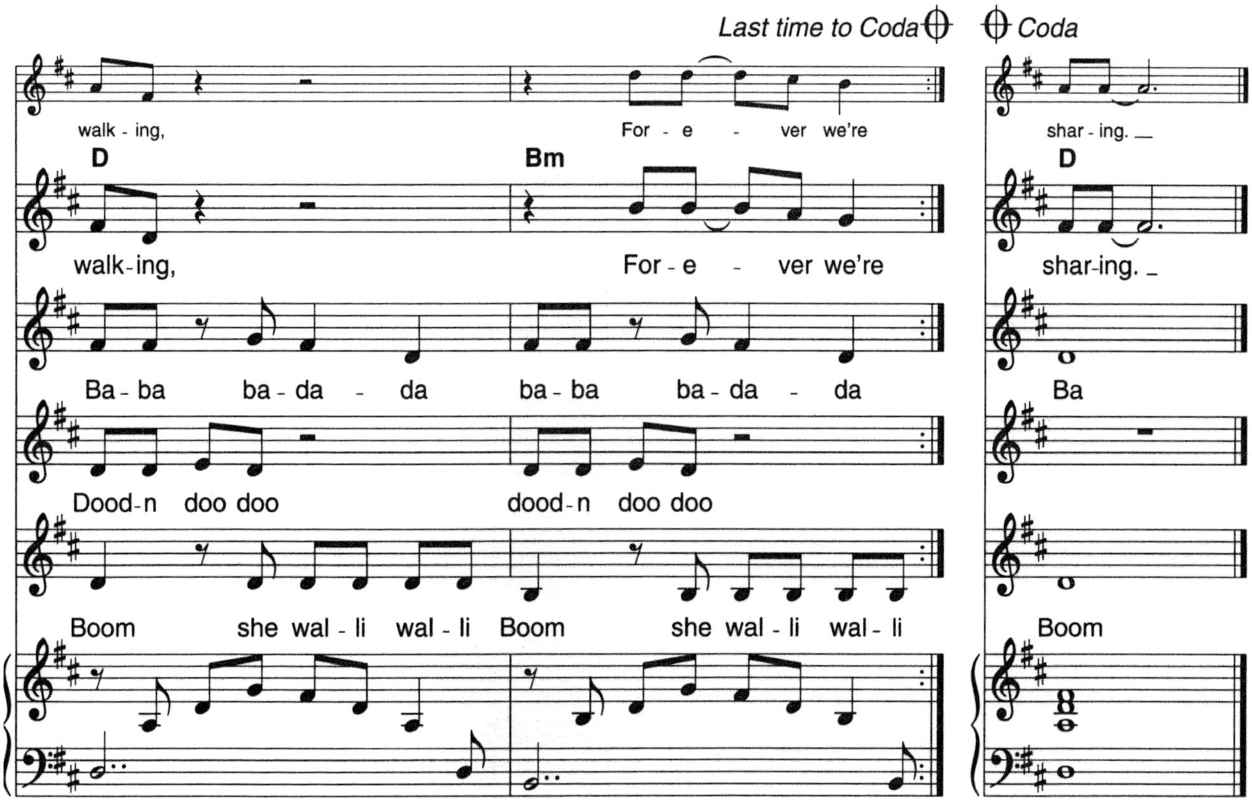

30 Project Layers

Hymn for the earth

Patrick Allen

30 Project Layers

Pupil's sheet

Keep moving forward

(Traditional/Words: Patrick Allen)

Keep moving forward,
Follow the guiding light.
Keep marching onward,
We know our future's bright.
Don't look behind you,
Good times will find you.
Moving forward – off we go!

Chord format

4/4

1	2
D Bm	Em A :

The fourth circle

(Patrick Allen)

1 Moving, all things are changing,
The earth is spinning and time is marching along.

2 All things are moving, all things are changing,
The earth is spinning and time is marching.

3 All things move, all things change,
Earth will spin, time marches on.

Chord format

4/4

1	2	3	4
Cm Fm7	B♭ E♭maj7	A♭ D^{dim}	G7 Cm :

Tina singu

(Lesotho)

1 Tina singu leluvateo, Tina singu leluvateo (x 2)

2 Watsha, watsha, watsha, watsha, watsha (x 2)

3 La, la etc

Chord format

4/4

1	2	3	4
D	Em7	F♯m/A A7	D :

Note: When a chord is written thus: F♯m/A the chord of F♯ minor is played with an A in the bass.

Percussion

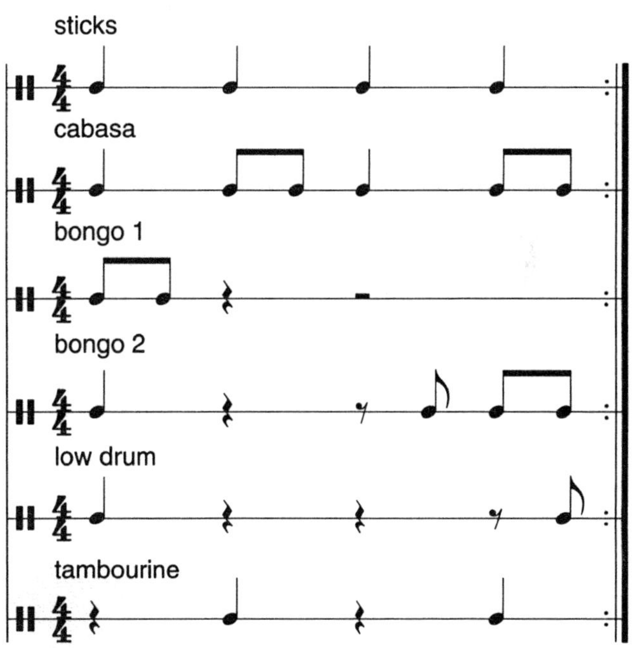

30 Project Layers

Pupil's sheet

Freedom highway

(Patrick Allen)

1 Walking together down the freedom highway,
No one we meet can take our freedom away.
We are walking, together we are walking,
Forever we're …

2 Walking together down the friendship highway,
No one we meet can take our friendship away.
We are walking, together we are walking,
Forever we're …

3 Sharing our freedom on the people's highway,
To all that we meet we give our freedom away.
We are sharing, together we are sharing,
Forever we're …

4 Sharing our friendship on the people's highway,
To all that we meet we give our friendship away.
We are sharing, together we are sharing
Forever we're … sharing.

Chord format

4/4	1	2 (Coda)
	D Bm :‖	D

Hymn for the earth

(Patrick Allen)

Ostinato backings

1 Children of the sun, we shall live as one. Take us to the light, sunrise steals the night.

2 Winds are blowing, waters flowing, make a new start, rainbow in your heart.

3 Climb the hills, search for the sea. Watch the waters flowing free.

4 Sunshine beaming on the earth, raindrops giving nature birth.

Verse

1 Earth that gives for all to share,
Sunlight, water, food and air,
Land and rivers, winds and tides,
Nature gives and nothing hides.

2 Man has come to plough the land,
Oak and ash fall at his hand,
Land and ocean give their store,
Mankind takes and asks for more.

3 Living on this common ground
We must care for what we've found,
Catch the rainbow in your soul,
Hope and love will conquer all.

Chord format

4/4	1	2	3	4
	♩ ♩ 𝅗𝅥	♩ ♩ 𝅗𝅥	♩ ♩ 𝅗𝅥	♩ ♩ 𝅗𝅥
	B♭ C F	Gm A7 Dm	B♭ C F	Gm A7 Dm

Rounds

The next pages contain a collection of twelve rounds from traditional sources, transposed to keys appropriate to the 11–14 age group.

Teaching the rounds

Teach the whole class the tune first, with chordal and melodic accompaniment if necessary to keep the class in pitch. Accompaniments for each round are suggested as follows:

- single note ostinato
- chords
- drone.

Once the class know the round, divide the group in half and stagger the entries as indicated by the numbers in circles. Subdivide further if you can, but rounds are often more difficult than they appear so don't be disappointed if you only manage to divide the class into halves or thirds.

Performing the rounds

Unaccompanied performance is the ideal but many classes will need the accompaniment when performing the rounds. When pupils are concentrating on their own parts they may not hear the full effect, so tape-record the performance so they can hear and evaluate their efforts.

Canoe round

Margaret Embers McGee 1918

Accompaniment: D drone

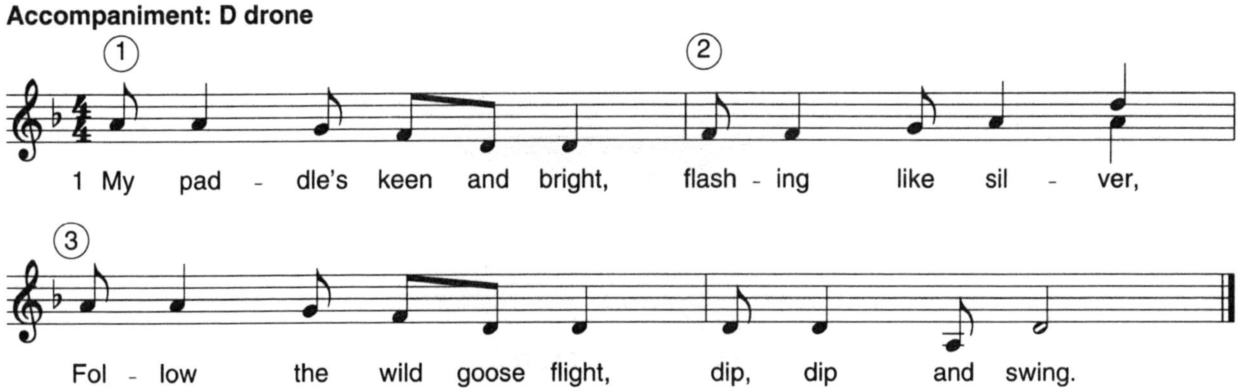

2 Dip, dip and swing her back, flashing like silver,
Follow the wild goose track, dip, dip and swing.

Sing this song

Accompaniment: chords

Rounds

Make new friends

Accompaniment: D A **ostinato**

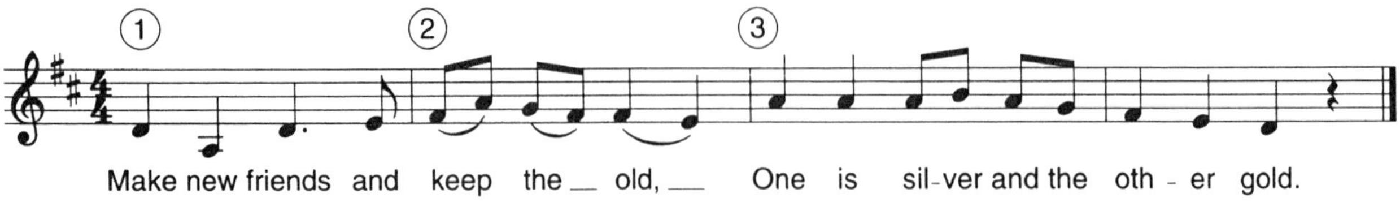

Row, row your boat

Accompaniment: B♭ F **ostinato**

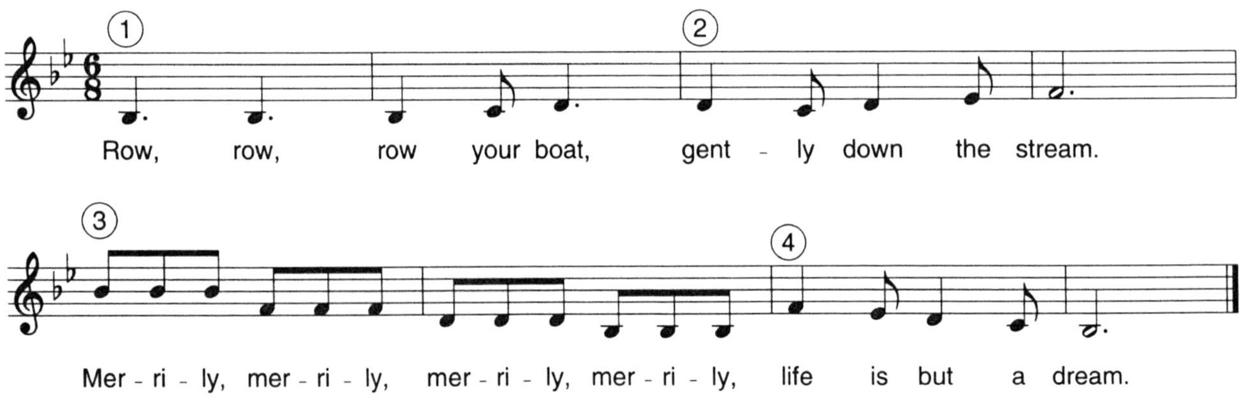

Goose round

Accompaniment: D A **ostinato**

Rounds

Hey, ho, nobody home

Accompaniment: chords

London's burning

Accompaniment: chords

Sing together

Accompaniment: chords

Rounds

Music alone shall live

Accompaniment: chords

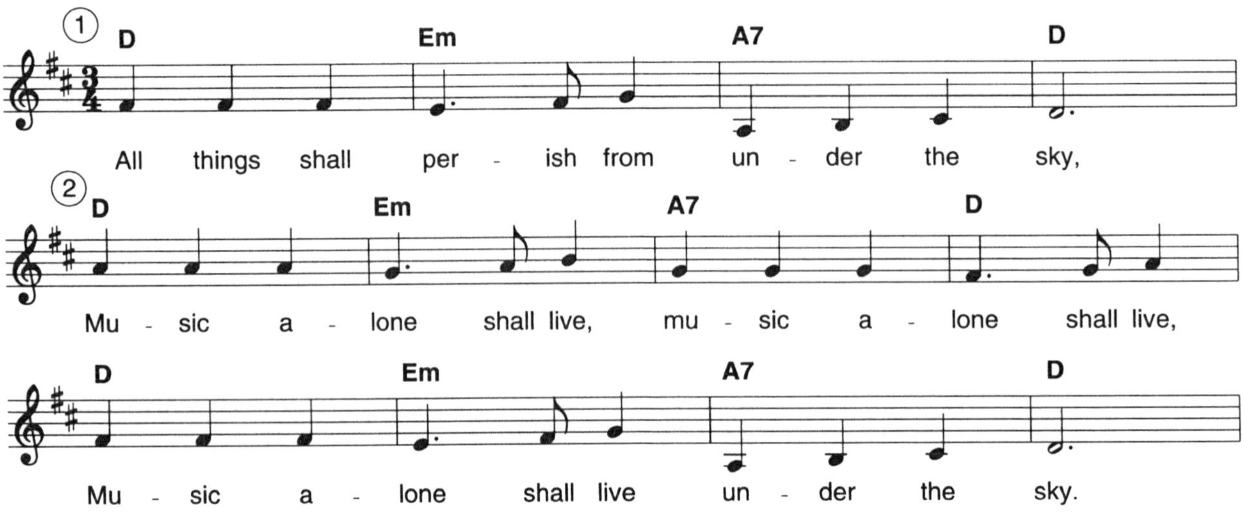

Follow on

Accompaniment: chords

Rounds

Bottle of pop

Accompaniment: chords

Note: This can be sung as a round or in layers.

Rounds

Kookabura

Australian (from a campfire song book)

Accompaniment: chords

2 Kookaburra sits in the old gum tree,
Eating all the gum-drops he can see,
Stop kookaburra, stop kookaburra,
Leave some there for me.

3 Kookaburra sits in the old gum tree,
Counting all the monkeys he can see,
Stop kookaburra, stop kookaburra,
That's not him that's me.

Chants

The following pages provide a collection of short chants which can be used as singing warm-ups or as exercises for developing particular skills. Some of the chants can also be effectively developed into performance pieces.

Tumba chant

Traditional arr. Patrick Allen

Note: Begin with ostinato A and gradually add B and C. Start the piece very slowly and eventually take it as fast as you can.

Sledging

Russian arr. Patrick Allen

Sing to 'lah'

Note: This Russian song is good for practising singing in 3rds and should get gradually faster. Melody 3 is a simple counter-melody.

Chants

Hava nagila

Israeli traditional

Note: This song is in the style of the 'Hora', a Yiddish dance.

Napoléon

French traditional

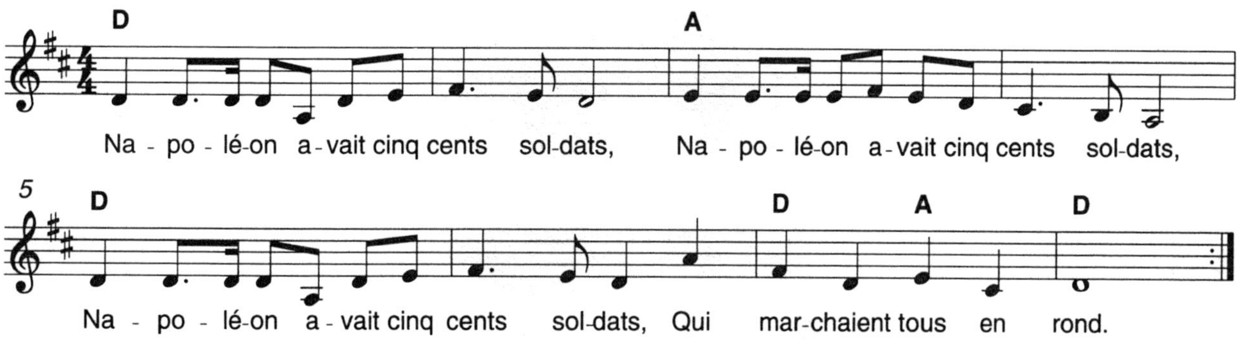

Note: This song loses words each time it is repeated. Firstly 'soldats', then 'cents', then 'cinq' and so on until there is silence! 'Qui marchaient tous en rond' never disappears. If sung in a circle pupils can march on the spot, or round the circle.

Hari Krishna Hari Rama

Hindu chant

Note: This Hindu chant is a bhajan. In this the congregation sings after a leader. The music starts very slowly but gets faster as it is repeated, ending up very fast.

Chants

Govinda

Hindu chant

Note: Another bhajan, the Sanskrit words mean: 'I worship Govinda, the primeval Lord.'

St Magnus

Patrick Allen

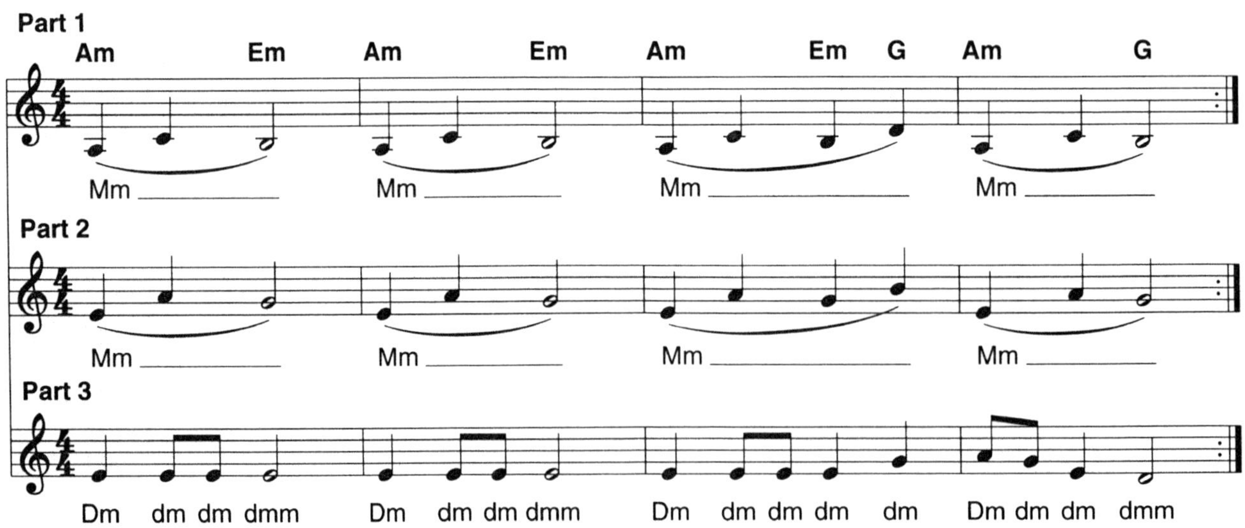

Note: This is a slow, meditative chant which can be sung with or without accompaniment.

Chants

The grand old Duke of York

English traditional

Note: Although apparently childish, this song works well when sung in a circle. It allows for simple movements as a response to the words, such as marching on the spot and round the circle, stretching up and crouching down and a variety of hand movements. In this respect it is a good song for relaxing the body and releasing inhibitions.

O sole mio

Eduardo di Capua/Words: Patrick Allen

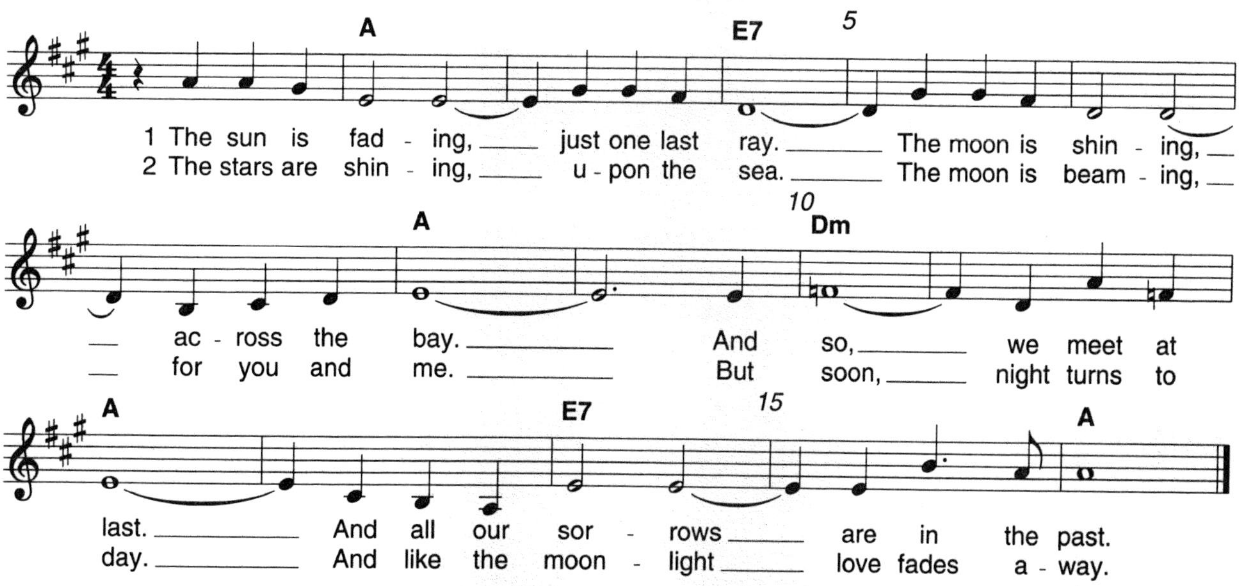

Note: This is a song which encourages 'mock-operatic' singing from pupils!

Chants

Can can

Offenbach

Note: This well known tune is good for relaxing the atmosphere and getting people to sing.

Mass chant

Patrick Allen

Chants

Percussion

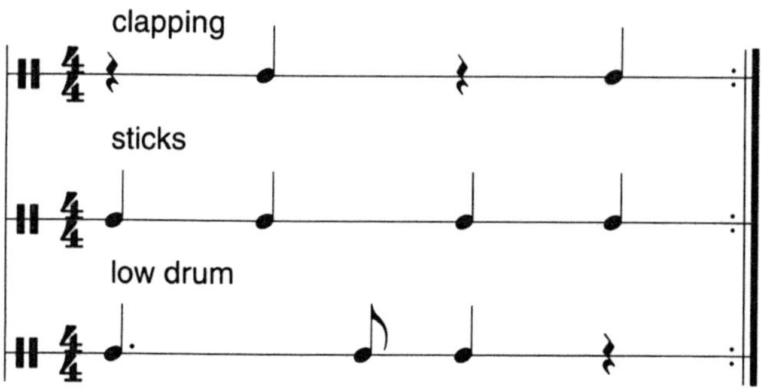

Note: This is a chant for a very large number of people. A firm drone needs to underlie the chanting and a clearly defined pulse. Experiment with varying the dynamics of each group so that each chant has its turn in the foreground. Teach the whole piece aurally.

Social songs

The next few pages provide a collection of songs which pupils may need to know in a variety of social settings. They include significant songs from the countries within the British Isles.

Abide with me (Eventide)

W. H. Monk (1823–89)/Words: Henry Lyte 1820

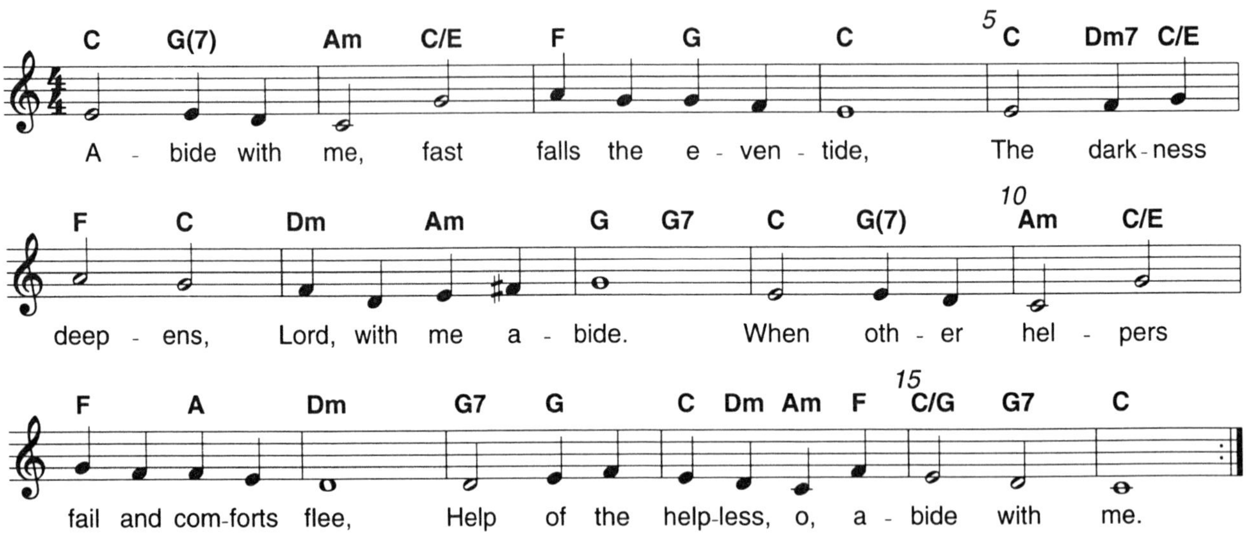

1 Abide with me, fast falls the eventide,
The darkness deepens, Lord, with me abide.
When other helpers fail and comforts flee,
Help of the helpless, o abide with me.

2 Swift to its close ebbs out life's little day,
Earth's joys grow dim, its glories pass away.
Change and decay in all around I see,
O Thou who changest not, abide with me.

3 I need thy presence every passing hour,
What but thy grace can foil the tempter's pow'r?
Who like thyself my guide and stay can be?
Through cloud and sunshine, o abide with me.

4 I fear no foe, with thee at hand to bless,
Ills have no weight and tears no bitterness.
Where is death's sting, where grave thy victory?
I triumph still if thou abide with me.

5 Hold thou thy cross before my closing eyes,
Shine through the gloom and point me to the skies,
Heav'n's morning breaks and earth's vain shadows flee,
In life, in death, o Lord, abide with me.

Social songs

All through the night (Ar hyd y nos)

Welsh traditional/English words: Harold Boulton

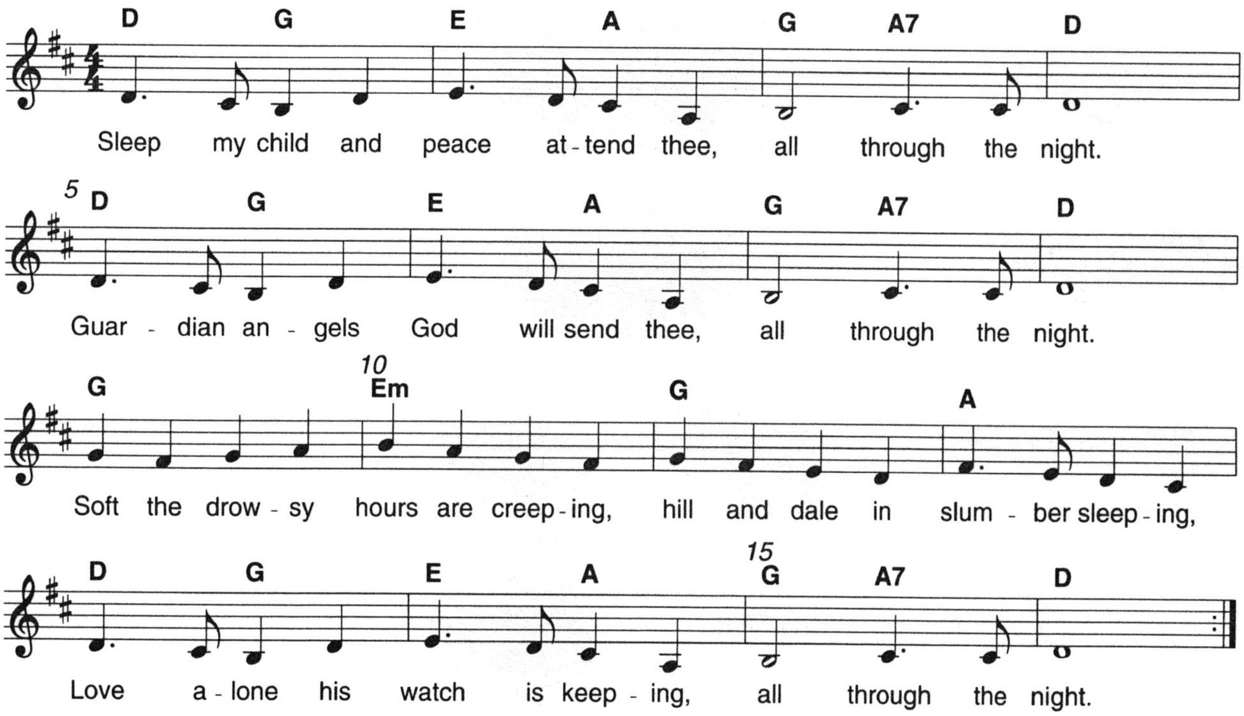

English

1 Sleep my child and peace attend thee,
all through the night.
Guardian angels God will send thee,
all through the night.
Soft the drowsy hours are creeping, hill and dale in slumber sleeping,
I my longing vigil (Love alone his watch is) keeping, all through the night.

2 While the moon her watch is keeping,
all through the night.
While the weary world is sleeping, all through the night.
O'er thy spirit gently stealing, visions of the light revealing,
Breathes a pure and holy feeling, all through the night.

Welsh

1 Holl amrantau'r sêr ddywedant, Ar hyd y nos,
'Dyma'r ffordd i fro gogoniant', Ar hyd y nos.
Golau arall yw tywyllwch, i arddangos gwir brydferthwch,
Teulu'r nefoedd mewn tawelwch, Ar hyd y nos.

2 O mor siriol gwena seren, Ar hyd y nos,
I oleuo'i chwaerddaearen, Ar hyd y nos.
Nos yw henaint pan ddaw cystydd,
Ond i harddu dŷn a'i hwyrddydd.
Rho'wn ein goleu gwan i'n gilydd, Ar hyd y nos.

Social songs

Amazing grace

Traditional (from *Virginia Harmony*)/Words: John Newton (1725–1807)

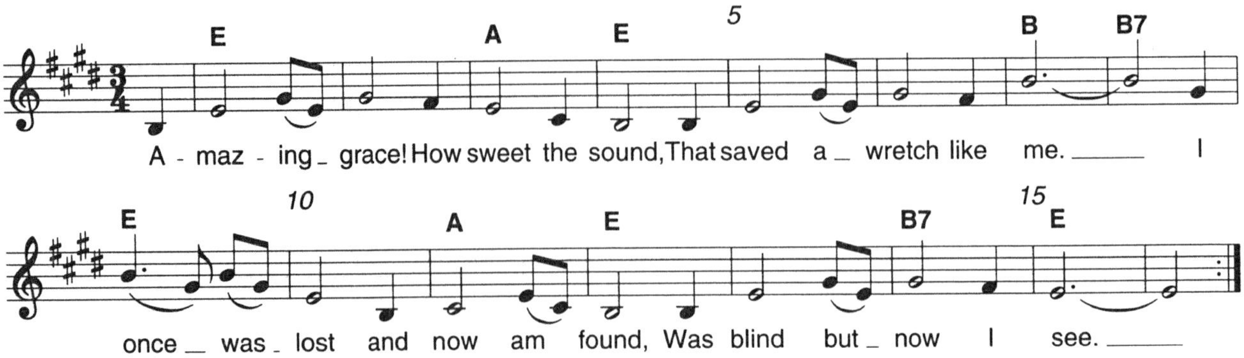

1 Amazing grace! How sweet the sound
That saved a wretch (soul) like me.
I once was lost and now am found,
Was blind but now I see.

2 'Twas grace that taught my heart to fear
And grace my fears relieved.
How precious did that grace appear,
The hour I first believed.

3 The Lord has promised good to me,
His word my hope secures.
He will my shield and portion be
As long as life endures.

4 Through many dangers, toils and snares
I have already come.
'Tis grace that brought me safe thus far
And grace will lead me home.

5 When we've been there ten thousand years
Bright shining as the sun,
We've no less days to sing God's praise
Than when we first begun.

Note: Newton was a slaveship captain who experienced a conversion on his way from Africa to America. He returned to Africa and set free his human cargo.

Social songs

Auld lang syne

Scottish traditional/Poem: Robert Burns

1 Should auld acquaintance be forgot and never brought to mind?
Should auld acquaintance be forgot and days of auld lang syne?
For auld lang syne, my dear, for auld lang syne,
We'll tak' a cup o' kindness yet, for auld lang syne.

2 We twa ha'e ran aboot the braes and pu'd the gowans fine,
We've wandered many a weary foot sin auld lang syne,
Sin auld lang syne, my dear, …
We've wandered …

3 We twa ha'e sported i' the burn frae mornin' sun til dine
But seas between us braid ha'e roared sin auld lang syne …

4 And here's a hand my trusty frien' and gie's a hand o' thine,
We'll tak' a cup o' kindness yet for auld lang syne …

Note: Verses one and four are the most frequently sung.

Social songs

Bicycle built for two

Harry Dacre 1892 (2nd verse: anon)

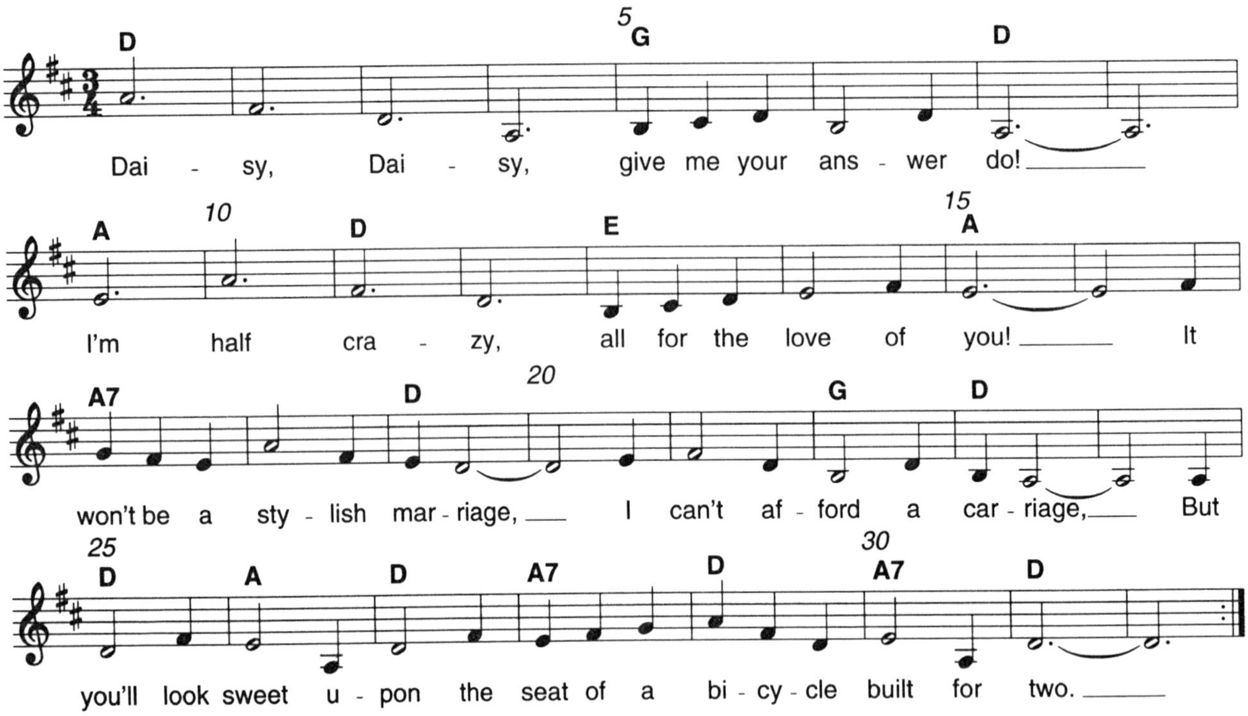

1 Daisy, Daisy, give me your answer, do!
I'm half crazy, all for the love of you!
It won't be a stylish marriage, I can't afford a carriage
But you'll look sweet upon the seat of a bicycle made for two.

2 Harry, Harry, here is your answer true,
I'll not marry, all for the likes of you.
If you can't afford a carriage, there won't be any marriage
And I'll be switched if I'll be hitched on a bicycle made for two.

Social songs

Danny Boy

Irish traditional/Words: Fred E. Weatherley

1 O Danny Boy, the pipes, the pipes are calling
From glen to glen and down the mountain side,
The summer's gone and all the roses are falling,
It's you, it's you must go and I must bide.
But come you back when summer's in the meadow,
Or when the valley's hushed and white with snow,
It's I'll be there in sunshine or in shadow,
O Danny Boy, o Danny Boy, I love you so.

2 And if you come when all the flowers are dying
And I am dead, as dead I well may be,
You'll come and find the place where I am lying
And kneel and say an *'Ave'* there for me.
And I shall hear, tho' soft you tread above me,
And all my dreams will warm and sweeter be,
If you'll not fail to tell me that you love me
I simply sleep in peace, until you come to me.

The flower of Scotland

Roy M. B. Williamson arr. The Corries

1 O flower of Scotland,
When will we see your like again,
That fought and died for,
Your wee bit hill and glen,
And stood against him,
Proud Edward's army,
And sent him homeward,
Tae think again?

2 The hills are bare now,
And autumn leaves lie thick and still,
O'er land that is lost now,
Which those so dearly held,
That stood against him,
Proud Edward's army,
And sent him homeward,
Tae think again.

3 Those days are past now,
And in the past they must remain,
But we can still rise now,
And be the nation again,
That stood against him,
Proud Edward's army,
And sent him homeward,
Tae think again.

4 *Repeat verse 1*

Social songs

For he's a jolly good fellow

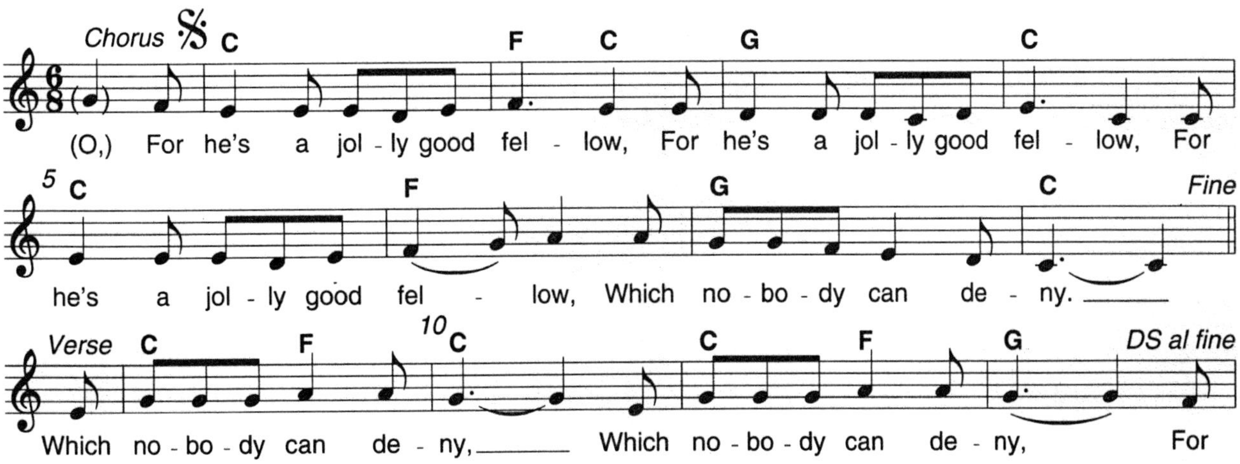

Chorus

(O,) for he's a jolly good fellow, (x 3)
Which nobody can deny.

Verse

Which nobody can deny. (x 2)

Note: This melody of ancient origin was first notated in the early eighteenth century as 'Malbrouk s'en va t'en guerre'. It has since been associated with a number of lyrics and was first printed with this one in London in 1901.

Social songs

Jerusalem

Words: William Blake/Music: Sir C. H. H. Parry

Note: Some pupils prefer this song transposed down still further, to the key of A.

Social songs

Land of my fathers (Hen wlad fy nhadau)

James James/English words: A. P. Graves; Welsh words: Evan James

English

Chorus (after each verse)

Wales! Wales! O but my heart is with you!
As long as the sea
Your bulwark shall be
To Cymru my tongue shall be true!

Verse

1 O land of my fathers, O land of my love,
Dear mother of minstrel who kindle and move,
And hero on hero, who at honour's proud call,
For freedom their lifeblood let fall …

2 O land of the mountains, the bard's paradise,
Whose precipice proud, valleys lone as the skies,
Green murmuring forest, far echoing flood,
Fire the fancy and quicken the blood.

3 For tho' the fierce foeman has ravaged your realm,
The old speech of Cymru he cannot o'erwhelm,
Our passionate poets to silence command,
Or banish the harp from your strand.

Welsh

Chorus (after each verse)

Gwlad, gwlad, pleidiol wyf im gwlad,
Tra môr yn fur
I'r bur hoff bau,
O bydded i'r heniaith bar hau.

Verse

1 Mae hen wlad fy nhadau yn anwyl i mi,
Gwlad beirdd a chantorion, enwogion o fri,
Ei gwrol ryfelwyr, gwladgarwyr tra mâd,
Dros ryddid gollasant eu gwaed.

2 Hên Gymru fynyddig, paradwys y bardd,
Pob dyffryn, pob clogwyn, i'm golwg sydd hardd;
Trwy deimlad gwladgarol mor swynol yw si
Ei nentydd, afonydd i mi.

3 Os treisiodd y gelyn fy ngwlad dan ei droed,
Mae heniaith y Cymry mor fyw ag erioed;
Ni luddiwyd yr awen gan erchyll law brad,
Na thelyn berseinid fy ngwlad.

Social songs

Old hundredth

1 All people that on earth do dwell,
Sing to the Lord with cheerful voice;
Him serve with love, his praise forth tell,
Come ye before him and rejoice.

2 O enter then his gates with praise,
Approach with joy his courts unto;
Praise, laud and bless his name always,
For it is seemly so to do.

We shall not be moved

North American traditional

Chorus

We shall not, we shall not be moved, (× 2)
Just like a tree that's planted by the water,
We shall not be moved.

Verse

1 We're fighting for our freedom, we shall not be moved (× 2)
Just like a tree that's planted by the water,
We shall not be moved.

2 We're black and white together …
3 We're young and old together …
4 We'll build a mighty union …

Note: Originally a union song from North America, but now sung all over the world to express solidarity and determination. It is based on an old gospel hymn inspired by a verse from the book of Jeremiah *in the Bible.*

Social songs

We shall overcome

North American spiritual

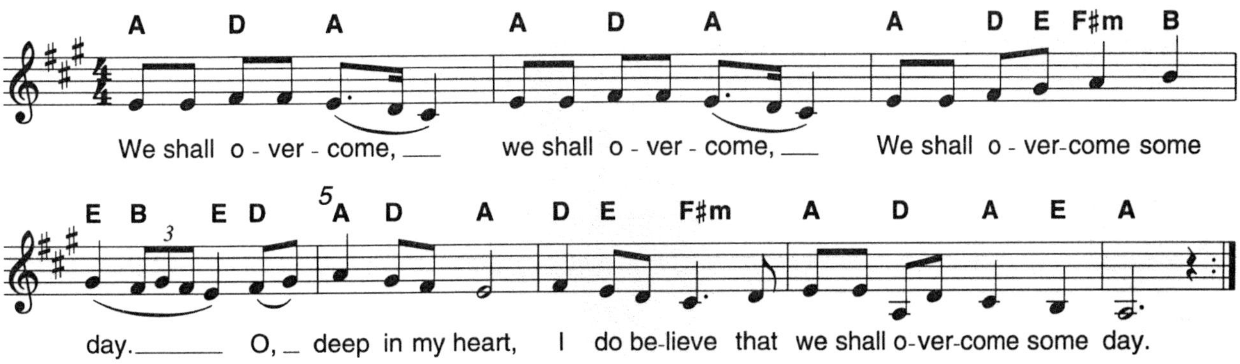

1 We shall overcome, we shall overcome,
We shall overcome some day.
O, deep in my heart, I do believe that
We shall overcome some day.

Verse

2 We shall all be free …
3 We are not afraid …
4 Truth will make us free …
5 We shall live in peace …
6 We'll walk hand in hand …
7 Black and white together …

Note: Based on the gospel hymn I will overcome*, this song of freedom and protest was first collected in 1946 on a union picket-line in Charleston. It has since then run the full gamut from gospel hymn to union song to civil rights chant to anti-war anthem to football song and back to Christian hymn!*

Social songs

Wild rover

Chorus (after each verse)

And it's no, nay, never,
No, nay never no more,
For I've played the wild rover
But never no more.

Verse

1 I've been a wild rover for many a year
And I've spent all my money on whiskey and beer,
Now I'll save up my wages, keep my money in store,
I never will play the wild rover no more.

2 I went to an alehouse I used to frequent
And I told the landlady my money was spent,
I asked her to trust me, her answer was 'Nay
Such custom as yours we can get any day'.

3 Then out of my pockets I took sovereigns bright
And the landlady's eyes opened wide with delight,
She said 'I've got whiskeys and wines of the best
And the words that I said, sure were only in jest'.

4 'You can keep all your whiskey and your beer likewise too,
For not another penny am I spending with you,
For the money I've got, I'm taking good care
And I never will play the wild rover no more.

5 If I had all the money that I left in your care
It would plough all my lands and my family rear,
It would thatch all my houses, it would build me a barn,
It would buy me a coat for to keep my back warm.

6 I'll go home to my parents and I'll tell what I've done,
And I'll ask them to pardon their prodigal son,
And if they forgive me, as they've oft done before,
It's ne'er will I play the wild rover no more.